CLEAN SWEEP

Banishing Everything You Don't Need
to Make Room for What You Want

DENNY SARGENT

San Francisco, CA / Newburyport, MA

To my late father, Clement Denny Sargent, who
taught me about Letting Go and who bestowed upon me
early on the gift of Laughter, the universal banisher!

First published in 2007 by Conari Press,
an imprint of Red Wheel/Weiser, LLC
With offices at:
500 Third Street, Suite 230
San Francisco, CA 94107

ISBN-13: 978-1-57863-388-3

Cover and interior design by Maija Tollefson
Typeset in Granjon
Cover photograph © Cindy Kassab/Corbis

Printed in U.S.A.

Contents

List of Banishings Practices

CONTENTS

BANISHINGS OF THE HEART: EMOTIONAL BANISHING

BANISHINGS OF THE MIND: PSYCHOLOGICAL AND THOUGHT PROCESSES

SPIRITUAL BANISHING

Introduction

We in the Western world have excelled in amassing wealth and goods, opportunities and responsibilities, technologies and information. Things, ideas, and sources of stress overwhelm us and overflow our lives, numbing our senses. We are constantly driven by a consumer impulse that simultaneously propels and supports our economy while imprinting endless desires and needs in our minds. We must have the newest gadget, the newest kind of food, and the newest information. As a culture we are driven to acquire, amass, get, use, devour, taste, and try.

As we want and amass more, we must work more. We have to do these things at the same time, though logic tells us that this means doing none of them with full concentration. There are too many errands, too much work, too many obligations, and not enough time. We are so deeply immersed in this frenetic ocean hyperactivity that we think it is normal.

A majority of people know that *something* is out of kilter, but most feel powerless to change. What would bring balance, control, and peace back to your life?

Those of us who travel outside the industrialized West (or even in some of its saner, quieter corners) know that most people in the world do not simply take and take. Many cultures have a sense of balance, an idea that one takes and then gives, that things are released so that other things can be gained. Just as day and night, activity and rest, consuming and excreting are all natural processes, so too in most cultures is giving and taking a natural cycle.

We in the west are very good at taking, consuming, hoarding, devouring, but we have forgotten how to let go, how to eliminate. We need to remember the basic concept of releasing and renewing.

We need to relearn how to banish.

What Is Banishing?

The *Oxford English Dictionary* says "to banish" means "to get rid of; drive away." An alternate definition is "to expel, as if by official decree." The root word, ban, indicates a much more primal and magical action. It means to forbid something, but in an active manner—that is, to exclude or consciously remove a person or action from society or a specific place. It also means "to speak."

Words are power. If you know the name of a thing or person, then you have control over it, you have power to manipulate it. All magical processes and shamanic rituals center on this idea. In many spiritual cultures, a priest, shaman, or other magic maker derives power from knowing the hidden names of things. For example, a shaman can call deer to the hunters by knowing the secret name of the animal. A priest can bring a god or spirit to a ritual by uttering words of power, and wizards conjure spirits by knowing their "true" names.

Banishing assumes that we all have the power to speak with authority, to take control of aspects of our reality by first clearly conceptualizing them and then uttering a directive to forbid, order, or prohibit it—to ban it from our reality by saying its true name or essence. In other words, by speaking or commanding, by conceptualizing we have the power to get rid of something—to send it away and keep it away.

To banish something, you must be able to name it—to get a hold of it and visualize it, to know it and thus have power over it. The fastest way to do this is to objectify or personify it. You may think of the thing you want to banish as a negative force, energy, or even an entity, such as a "demon," depending on your belief system. To me, for example, alcoholism is a "demon." Chances are that you have a number of "demons"—hurt, stress, pain—affecting your physical, emotional, and mental realities that you would be better off without. Banishing is casting out those "demons."

This book brings the idea of banishing into a simplified modern form. For our purposes, banishing means **identifying people, things, forces, feelings, thoughts, or ideas that are negative or harmful and, through the strength of will and positive power (love), commanding that these things be removed.**

As I wrote my previous books and articles, and traveled extensively, I became fascinated with the differences between philosophical religions and models and natural or organic models. With the help of people in Nepal, Costa Rica, Japan and many other places, I began to see that it wasn't just our removal from nature and the influence of Nature that affected us, it was the abandoning of the very basic biological model itself in our cultural hyperactivity.

The model is very simple: Any biological entity, from a single-celled organism to a human being, goes through processes that are cyclic throughout its lifetime.

• Food is consumed, digested and waste is excreted.

• Cells are created, mature, die, and are replaced with other cells.

Over the course of about six years, every cell in our body is replaced! Yet this is done in such a balanced manner, cell for cell, that we don't notice. If a cell overreplicates, copies itself too many times, it is an aberration and becomes a disease. We call it cancer. If an organism consumes but does not fully or completely excrete the waste, the organism becomes toxic and dies. Any botanist or biologist will be happy to spend hours telling you what a magnificent and endlessly complexly balanced dance this is and how even the slightest imbalance to an organism in this input/output, gain/loss system can throw the whole organism out of whack, leading to disease and multiple problems.

If you eat more than you consume, you get fat. This leads to a number of health complications that are quite well-know to everyone.

If you consume toxins or things containing poisons but do not fully eliminate waste and toxins, you slowly poison yourself. Again, everyone knows this.

If you keep acquiring (replicating) but don't give up anything or make room for the new . . . well, the biological model of overreplicating is cancer.

If this basic concept is applied to a culture as a whole, we have some interesting and, to me, startling images confronting us. A recent environmental study referred to the excessive rate of environmental destruction and habitat waste, being photographed by satellites, as looking like 'a cancer spreading' across the few wilderness areas left. We are very good at taking, consuming, hoarding, devouring, overworking and inputting more and more and more . . . but we have forgotten how to let go, how to eliminate. We need to remember the basic imprint of releasing and renewing that is imprinted in every cell of our body.

We need to relearn how to Banish.

Each of us is born with a True Will, an individual essence, reason we exist, a path we are meant to follow. When we are doing our True Will, we feel the universe is going with us; we are in the groove, we feel right with the world. This inner spirit or strength, I believe, comes from a higher power—call it a spark of God, gnosis, or guardian angel, if you like. Carl Jung called it the Self. The voice of our True Will is sometimes called intuition or our conscience. Things that detract or hinder/block your True Will need to be banished.

Throughout this book I use the term *love*, and I am mostly referring to a higher love, which often begins as self-love and self-confidence. This love keeps you rooted in this world and allows you to love others. Many negatives that you allow into your life or feel powerless to expel have roots in a lack of love. In the greater sense, God is love, as Albert Einstein said. Buddhists call this "compassion." Love is the key to everything. Love for yourself and for the universe is the basis of doing everything in this book.

Will without Love is simply aggressiveness and posturing; love without Will is passive and listless. Together, these two can move mountains and, with the right levers, can be used to banish almost anything from your life.

The Goal of This Book

The goal of this book is to help you shift you personal reality by introducing the concept of banishing into your life. The following chapters will explore the philosophies, ideas, and theories surrounding banishing in four main life areas:

The body and physical/material: negative attributes that are part of or embodied in your home, work, or living environment; in objects; or in your physical body;

The heart, emotions, and feelings: emotional relationships and attachments in your life or anything having to do with your emotional balance, health, or happiness;

The mind: mental attachments or obsessions, intellectual problems, mental addictions or excessive mental stress in your life, or anything having to do with your thoughts and thinking processes;

The spirit: attributes that are part of or embodied in your spiritual or energetic world, are part of your faith or are part of the unseen world that connects you with the divine, or anything having to do with your soul or spirit/etheric body.

Each chapter presents a clear path. You will find techniques and strategies powered by love and will to get rid of those things holding you back and making your life less than it could be. These techniques are drawn from a variety of cultures and traditions and organized by the very ancient concept of the five elements: air, fire, water, earth, spirit.

Banishing clears a space or creates a vacuum. It gives you more room for growth. At that point, you can decide what to fill that place in your head, heart, or physical world with.

Choosing What to Banish

Before you can get rid of something from your life you need to know what has to go. This means taking time to examine your life as openly and dispassionately as possible, with an eye to eliminating things, people, ideas, attitudes, feelings, cycles, and ideas you either no longer need or that are harming you. Habits, ruts, patterns of behavior—all of these things can be enemies of change in your life, and the only way you can see what works and what doesn't work is by examining all of it.

Deciding what parts of yourself and/or of your life you don't care for, what can or should be accepted, and what can or should be banished can be hard. But here is a simple, logical exercise to help you.

Step 1

Take four pieces of paper.

Title one paper "Body/Environment."

The next title "Emotions, Self/Others."

The third title "Mind/Thoughts, Self/Others."

The forth title "Spiritual/Supernatural."

Now brainstorm all the negative forces, or "demons," that are affecting you. They may be physical things, feelings, thoughts, problems, or even other people.

Take your time; be as open as you like, you are merely making a laundry list of negative things in your life that you could possibly change. There is no planning at this point, just recognizing and becoming aware of stuff you may not even consciously be aware of up until now. Write it all out in single words or phrases without a lot of deep thought.

Step 2

Go through your "demon" sheets and cross off the negative forces or problems that you can accept and live with. You may, for example, have written "low pay," but you may also love your job and, upon reflection, be able to live with the low pay.

Step 3

Underline all the items having to do with other people. You may, for example have listed, "My boss always criticizes me" or "My lover insults me." Change the wording of these phrases to put "I" at the beginning of them. For example: "I am angry at the unfair criticism I get from my boss" or "I am hurt when my lover belittles me."

As you do this, some issues that seem to be one category might move to another. What looks like an emotional issue (being criticized too much) may, upon reflection, be a mental one (lack of self-confidence).

Step 4

Now narrow the number of serious issues or "demons" to no more than three per page. You have to start somewhere!

Step 5

Once you have whittled down your lists, transfer the "demons" to four new pages, each divided into four columns. The first column on each page is labeled "Life Area," the second "Demon," the third "Banishing Actions," the fourth "Results."

The rest of this book will help you fill in the second column—the actual actions that will banish each of the "Demons" you have identified. You will read about many different action steps, techniques, practices, and rites for banishing. The results? That's up to you.

On the following page are some examples from my own "demon" pages.

Life Area	"Demon" (negative)
Body/Environment	Overweight and out of shape
Heart/Emotions	Unresolved pain at being abandoned by a good friend
Mind/Thoughts	Excessive overwork and anxiety about work
Spiritual/Supernatural	A long string of weird bad luck, feeling hexed

Is my life now perfect? No, of course not. Do I now have a new set of things, feelings, and ideas to banish? Yes, I do—I'm working on my stuff right now. Is my quality of my life better? Yes, it is. Banishing— that is, unloading or purging or banning or letting go of things that cause pain and negative thoughts and feelings—is can be hard. It can be painful, and it is rarely easy. But releasing a negative leaves room for a positive. Once you have banished a "demon" (or banished the nega- tives around it), then you can fill the void with something good. In the process of deciding what you want to get rid of, you usually become aware of what you need instead. If you banish hate, it can be replaced by acceptance, if not actual love; impatience can be replaced by

Banishing Actions	Results
Body Elimination Banishing, Sweat Banishing, Banishing with Exercise, Banishing Excess Weight	Lost more than thirty pounds, gained muscle
Breaking the Sorrow Cycle Banishing, Banishing Fear, Letting Go of the Brambles Banishing	Severed emotional connection, end of pain, end of mental/emotional attachment, peace
Banish Compulsive Thoughts, Banishing Away Anxiety Meditation, Slowing Down: Banishing Hyperthought	Found new joy, accepted advice/other patterns
Smudging, a Good Luck "Wash Banishing," Banishing with Stones and Crystals	Major change for the better, generating good chi/luck, acceptance, less upheaval

patience; pain can give way to peace. Banishing is the process of life; it is merely one step in that grand evolution of your Self into something better—someone more balanced, more at peace in your skin and with your world.

Banishings of the Body and Physical Environment

When you touch a body, you touch the whole person,
the intellect, the spirit, and the emotions.

—JANE HARRINGTON

In many spiritual and philosophical traditions, it is said that the body is the temple of the soul. The basis of this chapter and of much of this book is the interrelationship between the physical and the nonphysical. Yet, no matter what you wish to banish or get rid of in your life, it all begins with your physical being and your physical environment.

Begin the entire process of banishing by first looking at yourself in a mirror. Relax. Really look and feel your physical being. Ignore your thoughts and feelings, self-criticisms, and that nattering inner ego voice for a time. Just *be* in your body. You have been given this vessel of flesh; what an amazing wonder it is. Even today no one really knows how all the many complex system parts of the body work as a whole. It is truly a marvel that is so close to us that we often ignore it.

As you begin the process of assessing your life, your emotions, your desires, your thinking and your plans, stay rooted first and foremost in your physicality. It *all* begins with the body. When looking at problems, issues, hardships, and anything else that you feel may be an impediment or barrier to your will, begin with how it affects you physically. When seeking those things, feelings, ideas, and processes that you wish to banish or eliminate from your life, begin with your own body.

Without belaboring the point, your physical actions (or nonactions) are the easiest, most direct and most doable mode of banishing there is. Emotional or mental ills can often be banished with some exercise, diet, physical work, or a physical cleansing.

Spiritual work, in almost every culture, always begins with a physical clearing, cleaning, or banishing action. It may be as simple as a series of physical postures and breathing, like in yoga. Or a water cleansing of the hands, mouth or face, something most temples, shrines, and other houses of worship insist upon before one can enter and do spiritual practices.

A polluted or dirty living space leads to negative feelings, thoughts, and expressions. Dietary shifts almost always reflect in physical shifts, which reflect in emotional, mental, and even spiritual shifts.

So, no matter why you are reading this book and no matter what you think your problems may be, begin with your body. How do you feel? What parts of your physical life are you promoting or neglecting? If your mindset says you do not have time to maintain a healthy body, then nothing you do will set things right. Banish issues that negatively impact your physical being and surroundings and, amazingly, other more abstract problems will fade away. At the very least, setting a firm foundation of a balanced and acceptable physicality will allow you to focus on other emotional, mental or spiritual "demons" that you will to banish!

Air: Breath, Air, and Scents

We can live without water for three to four days, we can live without food for ten days or more, we can even live without excreting waste for a few days, but our life without breath can be measured in minutes.

Our lungs are where we renew ourselves every fifteen minutes or so. The expulsion of the carbon dioxide we do not need and the inhalation of the oxygen we do sets the rhythm of our entire body. In yoga, the vital air that we inhale does more than enrich our blood and feed our whole body with life-giving oxygen and other elements; it also brings vital energy into our body and so infuses our whole organism with what is called prana.

Many physical, emotional, and mental complaints and problems can be traced to poor breathing. If you feel a lack of energy, a lack of physical ability, and an overall fatigue, look first to your breathing. Short, gasping, or shallow breathing is indicative of a negative state of mind and body.

Close your eyes, sit, and breathe for a few moments. Are you using your full range of breath? Are your lungs fully inhaling and exhaling? Most people, especially when stressed, do not completely empty their lungs when they breathe.

Take a moment to breathe in to your fullest extent. More. More. Now exhale to your fullest extent. More. More. You will likely be surprised at the amount of air that your lungs can hold and that can be exhaled. That last bit of pushed out air when you fully and completely exhale is called stale air by some health practitioners. Coming from the very bottom of the lungs, it is often not fully exhaled and thus stays in the lungs, not being renewed.

The quality of our air is just as crucial to us as the action of breathing. Poor or polluted air accounts for a number of health issues, such as asthma and toxin-related illnesses. It is crucial that you measure the air quality around you and do what you can to improve it. Removing molds, for example, can clear up a number of severe physical problems. Moving to a place that is less polluted, planting more greenery around you, installing and maintaining air filters or purifiers—all of these may help alleviate health issues.

Simply getting outside and breathing the fresh air of nature can banish all sorts of stress-related problems. Physical exercise is important, in part, because it prompts us to take deep, oxygen-rich, lung-clearing breaths, which help revitalize our bodies.

In addition to oxygen, our lungs can bring other banishing agents into our bodies. My wife's inhaler, for example, banishes her bouts of asthma. Other sorts of fumes or smoke have been used for centuries to banish body issues. Certain herbs, when smoked, open the lungs and bring healing to the body. Sage comes to mind, but ancient texts and traditions are full of many different healing smokes used for banishing illness.

Airing out the house is something done in every culture, and it has very real benefits. Oxygen kills many kinds of fungi and bacteria, so bringing fresh air into your physical environment when cleaning removes sources of illness; it is also psychologically and emotionally healing.

Our air includes not just oxygen but also scents, and aromas have been shown to affect physical, psychological, and mental moods and feelings. Scents can depress or stimulate us, making us feel sluggish or energized. Hard research on aromatherapy confirms that scents can indeed banish negative feelings. One study from the University of Miami School of Medicine, for example, tested how subjects reacted to the scents of lavender and rosemary. The adults who smelled lavender showed increased drowsiness, but were also able to perform math functions more quickly and accurately than before they received the lavender; they also reported feeling relaxed. Those who smelled rosemary, on the other hand, displayed increased alertness and had lower anxiety test scores, in addition to being able to perform math functions more quickly. In other words, the lavender scent banished stress and the rosemary scent banished anxiety.

Pranayama

Goal: To banish all problems of the body through breath and thus power control.

Procedure:

1. Sit on the blanket, making sure you are calm and comfortable.

2. Breathe deeply for a minute or two. Let all your problems and ailments slip away for a moment.

3. Close your eyes, relax, and concentrate on the naturally calm rhythm of your breathing. When you feel you have reached a calm level of natural breathing, begin to focus on your in breath and out breath.

4. Breathe in to a count of five. Hold the breath for another count of five, then exhale for a count of five. Wait for a fourth count of five before breathing in again.

5. When you are comfortable breathing with this five-five-five-five rhythm, you may add a mental image. Visualize each expelled breath as grayish, smokelike energy that upon leaving your body and being is absorbed by the nature around you. See each in breath as filled with healing light, natural energy pulled from the lovely world around you. Continue this visualization as long as you like, until you feel refreshed.

6. When done, make thanks to the divine and nature, as you will.

There are many variations on this exercise, including some that focus specifically on emotional banishing. Pranayama, which literally means "life breath," is a vast and fascinating practice that can be further explored as you like.

Smudging

In essence, smudging is burning an herb or sacred substance to cleanse so that the smoke can banish ills. The herbs or substances that are traditionally used are sage, cedar, rosemary, pine, and lavender.

Goal: To banish the ills and troubles from a person or from a physical area.

Procedure:

1. If doing the smudging inside, make sure that all the windows and doors are open.

2. Say any kind of affirmation or prayer you wish.

3. Place the plants in a bowl or shell. With a cup of water nearby for safety, light the plants on fire. Let them smoke and smolder, but not burn. Wave a feather or fan or your hand over the bowl to direct and increase the smoke.

4. Circle the affected person or area counterclockwise, waving the smoke toward the person's body or about the room.

5. It is traditional to chant or say a prayer and to visualize the affliction/negative energy being forced out and up into the atmosphere by the smoke.

6. When done, offer the smoke to the divine and give thanks as you like.

7. Bury the ashes in the earth.

Healing Smoke

This Native American tradition has also been practiced, in many variations, in many different cultures for thousands of years. The herbs can be smoked without inhaling. Some commonly used herbs are:

Mullein	Said to aid all lung ailments
Horehound	An expectorant, will cause some coughing
Lobelia	To stop smoking tobacco
Sage	Promotes general health and a long life

Goal: To heal the body of specific ills. Can also be used to banish ills from an area.

Procedure:

1. Healing smokes are always better done outside, but if done to banish ills from in an indoor area or from both a person and an area, make sure all the windows and doors are open.

2. Put the herb in a special pipe or crush and roll it into a rolling paper.

3. Light the herb. Puff on the pipe or "cigarette" to inhale the herb smoke.

4. If you like, exhale some of the smoke upward as an offering to the divine. It is traditional to then offer some smoke to each of the four compass directions. At the same time, say a prayer, affirmation, or just a simple wish to rid oneself or the area of negativity.

5. As you inhale the smoke, picture the smoke entering your body and filling you with light. As you exhale, see the smoke carry away your problem as it fades into the sky.

6. When done, offer up any other prayers or good wishes you like. Put out the herb.

7. Bury the burned herb in the earth.

8. Relax or even lay down for a while.

Aroma Banishing

Though studies on aromatherapy do verify some common effects for scents such as lavender, scent preferences can be subjective. It is recommended that oils used or incenses used for aroma banishing be of the purest and best quality. Some may cause an allergic reaction, so test them first. Common aromatherapy scents include:

Musk   Helps with impotence and sexual dysfunction

Ginger   Brings warmth, helps with dizziness and nausea

Lavender   Calms, relaxes, decreases stress

Lemon   Increases energy, banishes the blues, helps mental focus

Sandalwood   Increases sensuality, sensitivity, and relaxation

Bergamot   Alleviates depression and overall system weakness

Sage   Promotes relaxation, opens the body to healing

Eucalyptus   Opens sinuses, eases breathing, helps with allergies

Geranium   Increases energy

Goal: To banish illness from an area or person, using various scents that cause physical, mental, and spiritual changes.

Procedure:

1. Thoroughly clean person or area with a scentless cleaner.

2. Sit calmly and mentally focus on the desired banishing.

3. Light the incense or diffuse the scent outward while offering an affirmation or prayer, as you like. Close your eyes and relax.

4. Wave your hand (or a fan or feather) to bring the scent toward your face. Inhale deeply through your nose. Let the scent pervade and fill you. See the scent as a bright light of whatever color you like, filling your body (or the area around you) with light.

5. As you exhale, picture the ailment you're banishing as a dark, grayish fume and consciously push it out of your body with your breath. Watch it disappear. Repeat as many times as you like.

6. When you are done, open the doors and windows and breathe the fresh air. Relax and empty your mind for a time before moving on with other things.

Many people continue the banishing by wearing or carrying small vials of the scent with them to smell and use as they need.

Fresh Air Renewal

Do this banishing on a nice, sunny day. You will need a number of nontoxic cleaners (cleaners with no chemicals), such as white vinegar in water, baking soda, and lemon juice; many stores carry a whole selection of commercial nontoxic cleaners. You will also need a selection of indoor plants.

Goal: To remove negative health influences and bring in healthy and healing air to banish problems.

Procedure:

1. Thoroughly clean all of your home with the nontoxic cleaners. Check all parts of your home for molds, mildews, dust, and dirt, which can affect air quality.

2. Make sure the fans and vents of your home are open, clean, and working properly, especially over the stove. Replace all filters.

3. Next, place an electric fan near an open window and turn it on. Open all the doors. As the house airs out, see light and joy enter your home with the fresh air. Picture negative energy flowing out the windows and doors with the old air, and see light and joy entering your home with the new, fresh outdoor air.

4. Hang or place the plants around the space. (See the Feng Shui Home Banishing practice in the fire section of this chapter for placement ideas.)

5. At sunset, close the doors and windows and sit. Breathe and enjoy. Notice the new feeling of peace and tranquility in your home.

6. Tend those plants and thank them for all the lovely fresh oxygen they bring you and your home environment.

Fire: Nervous and Digestive Systems

Your nervous system is the hardwiring of your body. It surrounds just about every other physical part of your body and plugs the whole kit-n-kaboodle into the operating system—your brain. Through the fiery flow of neurons, messages containing commands, data, and reactions race back and forth.

Most people already use medicine as a tool to banish pain or discomfort. Taking aspirin, for example, is a simple way to banish a headache.

How else can we use banishing to help our nervous system? One key way is by using a centuries-old Asian view of the nervous system as the meridians, or paths, that vital energy (called qi or chi) uses to travel throughout our body. As Phylameana lila Desy explains in *The Everything Reiki Book*, "The meridian healing system (originating in Chinese Medicine) is based on the concept that an insufficient supply of Qi makes a person vulnerable to disease. Restoring the Qi is the ultimate goal in restoring overall health and well-being to the individual." Using acupuncture or acupressure, we can manipulate the meridians corresponding to our nervous system, easing chi blockages and thus banishing problems.

Serious acupressure massage or acupuncture work should be done by a professional. But you can take charge of your own body (and its meridians) on the most basic of levels. You can change certain postures that bring pain by blocking meridians. Stress also blocks meridians, and you can often massage out these blockages by yourself. Getting someone to rub or even just touch you in painful areas can alleviate blockages and nervous-system issues. You can also wear clothes and shoes that do not restrict or injure your skin, and you can treat your senses and the nerves that connect them with care.

Just as acupuncture and acupressure fix chi issues in the body, feng shui fixes chi issues in your physical environment. It is believed that the environment and body are connected through the flow of chi, and negative chi in the environment leads to illness. Keeping the energy positive and flowing is key to a healthy physical environment, which in turn affects you. While this feng shui is a Chinese practice, similar arts can be found in India and elsewhere.

Under the rubric of fire we also find the flames of digestion, the system in charge of taking raw fuel and burning it to supply the rest of the body in its needs. Just as in any other part of your life, if toxins build up in the body, disease and problems occur. The digestive system includes the colon, bladder, and urinary tract, which banish liquid and solid toxins from the body. There are many who believe that the root of most physical ills lies in poor or clogged digestive systems. By choosing what and how much you put into your system, you help your system banish the negatives.

What you eat directly determines your health, and one of the easiest ways to banish toxins from your body is to watch what you eat and drink. In addition to avoiding caffeine, sugar, and wheat, three of the most common digestive-system irritants, you should also use healthy oils (such as olive and canola). Add whole or living foods, fresh juices, vegetables, and vital foods of all sorts to your diet. Drinking a lot of water is incredibly helpful for your digestive system. (See "Banishing with Nutrients and Food" in the earth section of this chapter for ways to use food for bodily banishing.)

Increasing liquid and fiber, has helped my overall health in many ways by banishing a lot of toxins; old, fermenting food; parasites; and more from my body's elimination system. Periodic colon cleansings can also clean out the digestive system, helping banish fatigue, weight gain, bowel problems, and other digestion problems. Digestive-system banishing also means taking time out of your very busy frenetic life to let your body release toxins. If you only partially evacuate your bladder, infections can occur. If you suffer from chronic constipation, toxins build up. While these problems are often dietary, they may also be due to stress or simply lack of patience with our body's functions.

Acupressure Banishing

Acupuncture is for professionals, but gentle acupressure can be used any time with a little forethought. Acupressure uses stress points, which are points on the human body where meridians of energy intersect. They are particularly sensitive. Many books and Web sites offer descriptions of stress points and explain their locations.

Goal: To banish negative chi and chi blockages from the body.

Procedure:

1. Find the stress point that is affecting you. For example, the stress point affecting a deep headache is located between the thumb and

the index finger. For sinus problems, several points are useful: one right next to the bridge of the nose, over just a bit on the cheek; another just above the eyebrow; another is the temple. One common stress point for a stomachache is between the bottom of the ribcage and the belly button. The stress point for an earache is in the front of the ear hole in the hollow that becomes deeper when the mouth is open.

2. Press gently on the tender stress point until there is pain, then slowly release until the pain has lessened.

3. Gently massage the point. Picture the blockages in the chi flow breaking up.

4. Repeat the sequence of pressing and holding, then releasing, then massaging the point until it is numb. Positive thoughts, chants, or prayers can help focus the mind and body when doing this.

5. Make sure you "earth" the negative chi, either by washing or by "throwing" the excess energy to the ground.

Note: Before going any further, an explanation is in order. The concept of *Earthing* is a crucial one in banishing. In this book it is defined as follows: To eliminate negative chi (bad energy) and remove it from a person, place, or thing by causing it to be absorbed by the earth, either directly or through the medium of water, a stone, or some other substance known for its ability to remove negative energy. You will find many references here to "earthing" negative energy. The point is to remove and dissipate such negative energies in such a way that the larger biosphere (the planet) can absorb them. In fact so-called "negative" chi or "negative" energy is simply misplaced energy. It is neither good nor bad.

You might think of Earthing as grounding excessive electricity. Just as a ground wire needs to be attached to power sources to let the electricity have somewhere to go, so we earth excessive or badly placed "negative" energy.

6. Relax and be still for a while.

Feng Shui Home Banishing

Feng shui is a complex art form and cannot be fully addressed here. But here are some basic fixes that can help anyone banish negative energy and stagnation.

Goal: To fix the areas of your environment that are leading to energy (chi) stagnation or are creating negative chi.

Procedure:

- In your living room, arrange seating so that people face the door when seated. If that is not possible, have a mirror doing so. This keeps the "chi" flowing. Circles and circular shapes are better than angles and sharp edges on furniture.

- In your home office, position the desk chair so your back is to a wall instead of toward the door.

- Stairs that lead directly to a door are not good; they lead all the chi to flow out the door. Hang a crystal or small mirror over the doorway, or place a table with nice items on it between the stairway and the door.

- In the bathroom, keep the toilet lid down and all drains stopped up to prevent chi from escaping through these fixtures.

- Use your bedroom just as bedroom, not as an office or for other nonbedroom activities. Your bed should not be in front of the door. Get rid of all clutter under the bed, and remove that TV.

- Get rid of clutter and piles throughout the house. They will get in the way of chi flow. Clean out drawers, cupboards, attics, garages, and all rooms. Eliminate everything that is not needed, that is broken, or that doesn't still fit. Even if you can't see the clutter, it is affecting you.

- Keep the kitchen clean, keep all pointed utensils put away, and use all the stove burners regularly.

- Use mirrors to keep energy circulating about your home, but don't put them facing your bed or anywhere you want to relax.

- Use crystals (often hung by strings) to redirect chi or stop it from draining away from a particular area. For example, it isn't good if your back and front doors are in line with each other. Chi comes in one door and flows right out the other. Hanging crystals over the doors helps the chi to stay. The chi hits the crystal and it refracts the flow of energy so that it flows throughout the home in an organic manner. Mirrors are said to do this as well.

- Make sure the colors you choose for your home feel comfortable and emotionally uplifting and are energetically appropriate for the rooms they are in. Rooms dedicated to entertaining or passion should reflect this with yellows, oranges, and especially reds. Calming, meditative rooms should be greens or blues. Notice your own responses to various colors. Your reactions are the key.

- Plants are great chi generators. They can add softness to a hard, angular spot or help keep chi flowing in corners or other places where it could stagnate.

Body Elimination Banishing

A little research on colon cleansing will show you that a dysfunctional digestive system can lead to many problems. This simple procedure is one of many ways to cleanse and to optimize your digestive system and thus banish the ills caused by a toxic system. It makes sense to combine this banishing practice with a shift in diet. You can also combine it with fasting.

Goal: To clean the digestive system of toxins and blockages, in order to bring about better health, weight loss, and better energy flow.

Procedure:

1. Stock your home with a variety of sugar- and chemical-free drinks, such as fresh juices (especially vegetable juices), filtered water, and herbal teas.

2. Buy a colon-cleansing mixture at a health-food store. It should contain psyllium-seed husks and a combination of herbs and clays.

3. Take the mixture as directed. Often you mix a teaspoon or two with juice and then drink it quickly. (Hint: Shaking the mixture and juice together in a glass jar works best.)

4. Be sure to keep yourself well hydrated throughout this process by drinking water and juices. For maximum effect, you would want to abstain from eating any solid food, but consult with your health provider before undertaking a fast.

5. After the first day or so, observe what leaves your body. It is truly amazing. If you like, you can pray and envision the toxins being expelled from your body during the cleansing period.

6. Continue to take the mixture as directed (usually 3 to 5 times a day) for a minimum of three days to a week.

Digestion and Consumption Banishings

If you are having stomachaches, indigestion, or other digestion problems, consider these ways to banish them. Always see a health professional if problems persist.

Goal: To remove digestion issues and to improve digestion effectiveness for overall health and healing.

Procedure 1: For a few days:

- Eat and drink nothing that has been cooked or processed—meaning nothing but raw vegetables, fruits, and nuts. Eliminate refined sugar and keep caffeine to a minimum.

- Drink only juices that are fresh.

- Drink herbal teas such as fennel, mint, or chamomile.

- Drink a lot of clear, filtered water.

Procedure 2:

1. Go to a good health food store and ask for acidophilus. Make sure to buy a type that is refrigerated and contains high-quality live cultures.

2. Take the acidophilus an hour or so before you eat. Picture the healthy bacteria entering your system, healing your stomach, and aiding the flow of energy into your body.

3. Stop eating all foods with refined sugar, white flour, and chemicals.

4. Continue taking the acidophilus and following this diet for a week.

Procedure 3: To specifically banish health problems like colds and flus, eat the following, if they agree with you: garlic; onions; hot peppers; mint, sage, or fennel tea.

Fasting Banish

Fasting is one of the oldest, most powerful forms of physical and spiritual banishing. In Eastern cultures, it is seen as part of the natural cycle of physical cleansing. Some health professionals recommend fasting for short periods of time at least twice a year. There are a few rules of fasting and it never hurts to add a spiritual element, such as meditation, prayer, and simply relaxing.

Goal: To give the digestive system a rest and to let it flush out stored toxins and clinging bits of food.

Procedure:

- If possible, schedule your fast for a time when you can take a break from your job and obligations. Avoid strenuous exercise or anything that requires much stamina or intense mental focus. You will experience a loss of energy and have less stamina (although some people actually feel more aware and energetic).

- Many suggest gradually beginning to fast—eating two meals a day for a bit, then one per day, then none. Others believe that simply ceasing to eat is the best way. It is up to you.

- When fasting, drink a lot of liquids, even if you do not feel thirsty, to help your body flush out toxins. Filtered water is best, along with healthy drinks such as herbal teas and vegetable juices. Avoid drinks with caffeine or sugar (or any sweeteners). Many people also keep fruit juices to a minimum because of the sugar content.

- Each day, take time to sit quietly and banish from your life those things you wish to let go of. You will enter a powerful and light-filled state of awareness. Use this state to make changes.

- Different people fast different lengths of time, but a recommended time is three days. Anything over that should be done only in consultation with a health professional.

- When you officially break your fast, usually in the morning, begin with something easy to digest and simple, such as soup. Progress slowly to simple solid foods. Do not chow down for at least a day or so.

Note: If you have any health issues or are pregnant or nursing, don't fast. Consult a health professional if you have any questions about it.

Water: Sweat and the Endocrine Glands

Water is the greatest source of purification we can find. We are, of course, mostly water, as is our planet. A surprising number of people are constantly dehydrated, and very few of us get all the water we need to keep our body functioning optimally. Our body's whole elimination system relies on a flow of water to carry away waste products and toxins.

The skin, largest organ of the human body, is key to healthy elimination. Its millions of pores regulate body health, and the most obvious way they can be stimulated is through sweating. Sweat lodges, saunas, steam rooms, and sweat-inducing practices have been staples of healing since time began. Many drug rehab programs make saunas and proscribed sweating a part of their detox process. Some of the things reportedly helped or banished by increased sweating include colds, flus, muscle and bone aches and pains, heavy-metal toxicity, sinusitis, and depression. (If you have any question about the stress excessive sweating puts upon your body, consult a health professional before attempting any of the practices in this book.)

Another recommended water-related method of body banishing is the simple bath. Baths help the body to efficiently eliminate toxins. The common bath can also be a very effective method of banishing stress and a host of other physical, mental, or emotional problems. Karyn Siegel-Maier, author of *The Healing Bath*, notes that hot baths can relieve arthritis and sore muscles, reduce hemorrhoids, and increase metabolism and circulation. "Cold baths," she says, "can relieve itchy skin, mild depression, asthma, and . . . rev up your waning libido."

Combined with oils, salts, algae, seaweed, minerals, and other elements, a bath can become a full healing ritual. A special bath also allows the body to literally absorb positive minerals, nutrients, and even herbal agents that can cause positive physical affects. Therapy baths are universal and often accompany many traditional or modern healing therapies.

While taking a "magical bath" is a passive and meditative banishing, the cleansing/washing process is active and energetic. One of the most common banishing practices in the world is using water—blessed, holy, or otherwise—to wash or cleanse away problems. On a purely practical level, cleaning the environment or the body removes all kinds of potential health hazards, from pollen to germs. On an energetic level, water grounds excessive energy, and, if the renowned Bioenergetics pioneer Wilhelm Reich is to be believed, it attracts orgone, or bioelectric energy.

The final water banishing has to do with the endocrine glands. The systems of glands throughout our body regulate everything from growth to reproduction. They are so complex that even today the science of endocrinology holds many mysteries.

Instead of examining their physical and chemical functions, let's look at the glands' effect on the whole body in terms of power and energy. For this point of view, we turn to the concept of chakras.

In the ancient Hindu tradition, chakras (meaning "wheels") are power centers said to emanate from the energetic body of each person. There are seven such centers, and they line up on the spinal column of the human body, beginning at the base of the spine and moving up sequentially to the top of the head. It is said that each center, from bottom to top, is more refined and vibrates at a higher level than the one below it. Each center embodies energetic keys for healing in proscribed areas of the body and in life. The purest center, our link to the ultimate divine, is located at the crown of the head. All the major glandular systems seem to shadow each center, and many people feel they are the physical root or basis for each chakra.

Center/chakra	Life area affected	Associated gland
Head/crown	Heals spiritual angst and hurts, depression, disconnected feelings	Pineal
Brow	Heals mental issues; develops mental faculties; increases intuition and is said to heal psychic abilities	Pituitary
Throat	Heals ear, nose, and throat issues, creative blocks or lapses, and speech problems and communication issues	Thyroid
Heart	Heals issues of the heart and lungs, emotional issues, and issues with becoming more giving	Thymus
Solar plexus	Heals digestive issues and organ/purification issues; said to be the center of the Will, so also heals issues of self-confidence, motivation, and drive	Pancreas
Sacrum	Heals sexual issues, including sex drive, impotence, and fertility issues	Gonads
Base of the spine	Heals lower-digestion problems and issues involving elimination and cleansing; also heals all body traumas and the body as a whole	Adrenals

For further study, I recommend the reader reference the many excellent books and Web sites on chakras.

Sweat Banishing

Goal: To relieve health problems, to detoxify and cleanse, relax and renew the whole body.

Procedure:

1. Focus on what it is you wish to banish. For example, when I get a chill or the beginnings of a cold, I immediately go to my gym and work out, then head to the steam room or sauna. As the heat covers me, I relax and breathe deeply while focusing on my whole body. I feel my temperature rise and feel my immune system go into action. It will be an individual experience, of course, I visualize all the "yuck" in my stuffed sinuses or scratchy throat as smoky-colored toxins. When I do the following exercise, as I sweat and exhale, I see this grayish yuck flow out of me, replaced by the bright reddish glow of an active immune system.

2. Go to the sauna or steam room and relax, letting your body adjust and sweat openly. It is best if you are naked, but if you must be clothed, wear as little loose clothing as possible and wear only natural fabrics.

3. As the sweat begins to flow, breathe slowly and deeply. Stretch. Feel all your pores open. Feel your ailment sweat away.

4. After ten to twenty minutes, leave and take a lukewarm to cold shower—the colder the better. Taking a cold bath or pouring a bucket of water over yourself also works.

5. Rest in a comfortable environment and adjust.

6. Repeat this cycle, as you feel comfortable.

Note: Including visualizations, meditations, and other spiritual-focusing techniques can greatly benefit this practice.

Hydration Banishing

Goal: To eliminate specific health problems and rejuvenate the whole body.

Procedure: For at least one week:

- Drink nothing but pure water. This may mean installing a filter system or having bottled water delivered.

- Eliminate sodas, caffeine drinks, sugar-filled teas and energy drinks, and so on.

- Eat properly, avoiding *all* refined sugar and as many chemical additives as possible.

- Drink at least ten 8-ounce cups of water every day, throughout the day. Yes, you will pee more often, as your body eliminates bad things. After a week, look back and meditate on how you feel and what positive changes have happened. Continue the procedure for as long as you like.

Note: Many people like to "charge" the water they drink with prayers, spiritual energy, crystals, and so on. Many people also swear by the affects of magnetized water—water that has had a powerful magnet immersed in it or that has sat on such a magnet.

Magical Bath Banishing

There are basically three kinds of banishing baths: one uses salts or minerals, another uses herbal infusions, and the third uses extracts or oils. Here are a few options.

- For a salt or mineral bath, use Epsom salts, sea salt, or any number of commercial mineral/salt therapy-bath mixtures.

- For an herbal bath, get some muslin cloth and wrap herbs in it. Tie it off with some cotton thread to make a giant tea bag. Or cut the herb fresh, tie the stalks together, and let them soak in the tub. Some traditional healing bath plants are fern, geranium, marjoram, mullein, rue, St. John's wort, and thyme. For relaxing, try chamomile, hops, lavender, peppermint, rosemary, or valerian. Hyssop has been used for hundreds of years; the Bible and other holy texts mention it as the supreme banishing herb.

- For an extract or essential-oil bath, a simple oil such as jojoba or coconut can be used.

    Goal: To alleviate or banish specific health issues and/or promote general health, rejuvenation, and well-being.

    Procedure:

1. Clean the tub very well with a nontoxic cleaner or just a little pure soap and water. Rinse.

2. Clean your body, opening all the pores. A shower works best.

3. Fill the tub with very hot water. If you are using a mineral or salt, slowly add it to the water as it gushes out of the tap, stirring a few times to make sure it all dissolves. If using herbs, place the herbs in the tub as the water runs. A few drops of oils or extracts can be added in the same way.

4. Let the tub sit until it is cool enough for you to enter, but still hot.

5. Turn the lights down or off. Light a candle if you like.

6. After getting in the water, spend a minimum of ten minutes in the soak. Many people soak for far longer. Do not use any soap. If you ever feel light headed or dizzy, stop and slowly get out.

7. While soaking, relax, meditate, and visualize what you are banishing from your body.

8. When you are ready to get out, make sure the room is warm. Dry off.

9. Lie down and relax afterwards.

Banishing Wash

Goal: To purify, clean, and banish unwanted physical problems from the body and/or home.

Procedure:

1. Clean your environment or body with water and a cleaning agent, such as pure soap or vinegar.

2. Prepare a special wash by simply boiling water or by adding a few drops of essence or scented oils to a bucket of warm water. To make a simple very positive-chi wash, put herbs in a bucket of warm water and sit the bucket in the sun for a few hours; then strain out the herbs.

    For an astringent body wash, use witch hazel or lemon juice in the water. For a therapeutic body wash, use lavender, sage, or rose water. For beautiful skin, add chamomile or mint.

For a home wash, add vinegar, lemon juice, bleach, or garlic to clean and help sterilize surfaces. Add lavender, lemon, rose, marigold, rosemary, or sage, whose scents promote positive feelings.

There are many possibilities to choose from. Just make sure the wash is pure and chemical free.

3. When you wash, using positive, spoken or mental affirmations, prayers, or chants can add to the effectiveness of the banishing.

Chakra/Gland Center Banishing

On a purely physical level, this practice can be used to open up or help facilitate the endocrine glands. On an energetic level, it opens and unblocks specific charkas or energetic body functions.

Goal: To promote overall body health, to unblock chi flow, to address health issues related to specific chakras, or to banish issues from the whole chakra system and open it.

Procedure: If you are working on yourself, you can massage the heart area on your body in a slow clockwise motion. If you are working on another—a much easier option—only the back is massaged.

All nonessential clothing should be taken off; anything worn should be loose and made of natural fiber.

The room should be warm, clean, and dimly lit. It is a good idea to perform a banishing procedure in the room, such as smudging, before such work.

1. Make sure your hands are very clean and that you are calm and centered. Clear you body, heart, and mind. Focus on the healing work. Pray or chant as you like.

2. Rub your hands together briskly until they are warm. Feel the energy build up in your palms.

3. If you are doing all seven chakras, begin at the crown of the head and work on each chakra until you come to the base chakra. Gently rub the physical area of the chosen chakra *clockwise*. Visualize positive energy flow from your hand(s) into the person. Mentally envision the blockage or problem flow away. Keep massaging until you feel warmth and you feel that the issue is resolving.

4. When finished, wash your hands, letting go of any negative energy collected. People often use salt water for this energetic cleansing.

5. After you are done, have the person who has been worked on take a short warm shower without soap and lie down for at least an hour.

Note: There are a number of sounds that traditionally are used with chakra work. Here is one set that is very effective and seems to help open up the various chakras. Consider gently chanting them as you move your hands over the appropriate chakra.

Chakra	Sound
Crown	Nnnggg
Brow	Mmm
Throat	Eee
Heart	Aayy
Solar plexus	Aahh
Sacral	Oohh
Base of the spine	Ohh

Earth: Flesh

The "earth" parts of our body—our flesh and bones—are the foundation of our physical being, the bricks, stone, and frame that supports and sustains all else. The way that flesh (including muscle, fat, and skin) and bones (including tendons and cartilage) interact is key to the way the rest of the body works. It is the most fundamental truth that how we treat out flesh and bones, how we create our physical form and maintain it, sets the tone for all other things in our lives. Just as a house (or temple) is only as strong as its foundation, so too is our body only as balanced as these elements are.

Often physical problems begin with a loss of, or a need for, specific nutrients or kinds of food. Helping the foundation of the body may also include adding to our diet minerals and vitamins that we may need. While this may not seem like banishing, the idea is to give your body X and thus banish problem Y, maybe even before Y becomes a problem.

Sometimes the problem is not that we lack something, but that we consume too much of what we do not need. Clearly, when we ingest more calories than we burn, the extra calories become fat stored in our bodies. When I was very overweight, the extra pounds put a strain on everything from my heart to my feet to all my internal organs. Casting off your excess weight is casting a "demon" off your body.

Exercise is the best form of physical banishing there is. It helps the lungs keep our blood fully oxygenated (air); aids digestion and the healing of the nervous system (fire); increases circulation, sweating, and overall flow of secretions in the body (water), while also aiding in the elimination of toxins; and builds healthy muscles and bones (earth). It also helps release endorphins and other brain chemicals that alleviate depression, shift moods, and even may help stave off conditions such as Alzheimer's.

Recent studies show that vigorous exercise, not just walking or strolling, several times a week, is really necessary for body health. This sort of exercise truly engages the whole body and gets all the organs and systems to work. Systematic stretching opens up all the muscles, increases circulation, and increases the flow of vitality throughout your body. Stress locks into the muscle, as do other mental or emotional traumas. The fastest way to banish these negative impacts is to stretch and send them out of the body. Yoga, tai chi, and similar forms of exercise also help.

Massage of all kinds is a powerful healing tool and can be found, in a variety of forms, in countless cultures. Massage promotes relaxation, the banishing of not just stress but also of toxins and calcification.

Banishing the Physical Environment

Often it is our very physical surroundings and environment that either leads to physical problems or which can make those issues worse.

Goal: To eliminate the physical basis of negative chi by removing physically harmful clutter items or filth.

Procedure: Do a serious and thorough physical check of your living space and physical area for sources of potential physical problems and eliminate them. For example, such a sweep caused me to eliminated old stored paint, all toxic lawn products, some faulty wiring and a nest of rats (!) from under my home. In my yard I had dead limbs removed from trees, corrected a minor yard-flooding problem, and repaired my fence.

1. As previously mentioned, clean! But also eliminate items (like a chair) that is simply too old or saturated! Get rid of any furniture that causes even minor discomfort. Turn your mattress over and get a new one regularly. Toss clothing, household items that don't really work, and so on.

2. Keep your closet free of piles and cramming; keep your garage organized and free of clutter. This is a huge one! Get rid of stuff!

3. The hardest: Organize! Clear out junk-filled drawers, shelves, and cupboards. Consciously decide where things should go, then change your behaviors so that you put things where they belong! One rule of thumb is to store things near where you use them.

4. Finally, keep a regular cleaning/organizing schedule!

Banishing with Nutrients and Food

Goal: To banish specific and general wellness issues with proper nutrients and food.

Procedure 1:

- Unless you eat remarkably well and all your food is fresh and natural, you should be taking good multivitamin supplements every day.

- Specific problems can be addressed with specific supplements. A common example that has proven very effective for me is zinc. Stress depletes zinc from the body and thus compromises the immune system. I take zinc when I feel a cold coming on, and it seems to banish 75 percent of those illnesses right away. A few other common supplements and what they help banish are:

Melatonin, valerian	Insomnia
Aloe vera, acidophilus	Stomach pain
Calcium, magnesium	Arthritis pain
B vitamins	Stress and tiredness
Cranberry extract	Minor bladder problems
Vitamin A and K	Eye problems

Note: This is not a medical book and not a substitute for advice from a health-care professional. Clear all vitamins and supplements with your health-care provider. Naturopathic doctors can also recommend specific supplements for specific ailments. It is always a good idea to do some research and get professional advice.

Procedure 2:

- Many of us have a number of unknown food allergies. Wheat, corn, nuts, and other items may cause adverse reactions. Try a gluten-free, casein-free diet for a while, if you can; that is, stop eating all dairy and wheat or wheat-derived products for at least a week. Many people find immediate health benefits.

- Switch to healthier (organic, if possible) meats and vegetables.

- Food additives, chemicals, and artificial flavors adversely affect a large number of people. For example, monosodium glutamate (MSG), a common additive, often causes health issues. If you are having health issues, read labels and avoid products with additives and preservatives.

- Eat regularly, and eat protein, vegetables, and grains.

- Cut down on fatty foods, sugar, and caffeine.

- Switch to healthier oils, such as olive and canola oils.

- Drink more water.

Banishing Excess Weight

Goal: To reach a weight level that you are comfortable with and that does not adversely impact your health.

Procedure:

- Start with a clear understanding about what *doesn't* work. Write down and think about all the diets you've tried and why they didn't work. But do *not* blame yourself or feel guilty. Simply write why the diets didn't fit your life and needs.

- Set a specific, realistic goal. "I want to lose a lot of weight" is no help. "I want to lose ten pounds this year" is both realistic and gives you a practical, specific time frame.

- Decide what you really will and will not do for the long term. If you are a sweets lover (like I am), saying you will give up all sweets forever will not work. But saying you will limit sweets and eat some kind of vegetable with every meal is doable.

- Keep track of what you eat. This may mean keeping a food diary, it may mean calorie counting, it may also mean becoming aware of what foods are loaded with what calories. A cheeseburger, for example, has way more calories than a banana, yet either might satisfy a craving.

- Be kind to yourself. Let yourself indulge, but do it in ways that won't torpedo your goal.

- Discover *why* you overeat. Often overeating is due to stress and emotional issues. Deal with those issues, and the weight loss may happen naturally.

- Exercise—even a bit every day helps.

Banishing with Exercise

Goal: To banish stress and other specific problems and to promote a general mental and physical sense of well-being.

Procedure:

- Schedule regular exercise times each week. Maybe you like to walk after work, visit the gym, or go to a yoga class. Whatever type of exercise you prefer, make it part of your regular schedule. Treat it like a doctor's appointment—something you cannot miss.

- Do only the exercise you are willing to do. Something you like is better than something you dislike, but you should never do any exercise you actively hate.

- Reward yourself after every exercise session, but not with food. For example, after I lift weights, I always allow myself time in the sauna.

- Start slowly. Work up to goals gradually. Don't be discouraged.

- Sweating is a healthy aspect of exercise. If possible, find a form of exercise that let's you work up a good sweat, or follow your exercise session with time in a sauna or steam room. (See the water section of this chapter for more on the benefits of sweating.)

- Drink *a lot* of water when you exercise and afterwards, because it helps the body banish toxins and fat.

- Use every chance to exercise. Take stairs. Walk to the store. Bike to work.

- Have a specific intense exercise you do when you are really stressed. For example, if you come home from work stressed and feeling bad, immediately get out and exercise before you collapse in front of the TV. A jog, a bike ride, or aerobic exercise will shake the stress off before it has a chance to settle into your bones.

- Include affirmations, prayers, chants, and creative visualizations in your exercise sessions. Use the time to focus on tossing the negative and invoking the positive.

Stone-Therapy Massage Banishing

There are many kinds of massage. Here is one technique that can help banish specific problems and is easy to do alone. Stone therapy, also known as thermotherapy, uses smooth hot and cold stones to apply heat, cold, and pressure to different key points on the body. It is specifically used to banish imbalance and specific ills linked to these different points.

Goal: To alleviate physical problems and issues, either specifically or in general, using cool and warm stones.

Procedure:

1. Collect a number of smooth, flat stones. Make sure they are very clean.

2. Place some in a bowl of cold water and some in a bowl of very hot water. Have a hand towel nearby to dry them.

3. After taking a shower, lie naked in a warm room. Find the spots on your body that seem to be the key to your problem.

4. Place a warm stone on the first problem spot. Explore the feeling it causes. After a few minutes, place a dried-off cool stone on the same spot. Again, open your mind and observe. Repeat, as you like. See what works and what doesn't. Research acupressure points and try using warm and cool stones on those key spots. If you have no specific trouble spots, try placing a stone on the forehead, the heart, and the lower belly.

5. When done, wash the stones and put them away to use another time.

The Spirit Body: The Brain and the Etheric Body

The Brain

In a lot of ways, many of the physical "demons" we want to banish reside in the brain, and the functions of the brain hold the key to the success of any banishing. Focusing the mind on such physical improvements as healing or weight loss has been proven to work. An entire issue of the *Journal of Consulting and Clinical Psychology* (July, 2002) documents well the role of psychology in the management of many specific physical problems and diseases. Psychological techniques such as visualization and hypnosis can, for some, lead to positive physical changes.

Because the idea of "mind over matter" is in many ways, the guiding principle of this chapter—and this whole book—it is important that we also focus on caring for our brain. The first questions you should ask yourself are:

- **Is my brain getting the right nourishment?** Are you giving it the foods, nutrients, and chemicals it needs to function?

- **Is my brain getting exercise?** Are you actively thinking, learning, adding to your skill set, or are you passively absorbing information?

- **Is my brain getting healthy and balanced stimulation?** Are you in sensory-overload mode all the time? Are you inputting too much media or computer stuff? Do you feel overloaded and burned-out?

- **Is my brain getting enough rest and relaxation?** We require a certain amount of sleep and downtime to function properly. Periods of calm reflection—meditation, if you will—and free cognition (daydreaming) are crucial to your mental health.

- **Is my brain getting the right training?** Mental organization and methods of keeping mental focus are learned, not inherent.

Techniques for exercising the brain and for focusing it on different stimuli will go far to banish certain problems. There are a number of body-mind exercises—such Tibetan eye exercises, Neuro-Linguistic Programming (NLP), voice/listening exercises, and right/left brain interactive exercises—that are excellent for sharpening the mind, increasing coordination, and banishing confusion and sluggish mental processes, and all kinds of imbalances.

The mental images we bombard our brains with can deeply affect our neurological state of being, which in turn affects our physical health. Just as you are what you eat, you are also what sensory input you take in. For example, studies have shown that "tech overload" directly contributes to irritation, aggression, depression, and other health issues. Banishing a cell phone or TV may be the most powerful and effective banishing you ever do; even limiting use of these devices can be very effective. Controlling technological and sensory overload can help us get rid of lethargy, minor depression, headaches, and any other chronic physical ailments that don't seem to have a concrete physical cause.

A number of health and lifestyle issues that call for banishing have more to do with the coordination of several physical things than just one problem here or there. Banishing issues that impact this part of our functionality call for more holistic methods. Practices that cultivate the mind as well as the body include yoga, tai chi, kung fu, and dance therapy. Buddhist monks do walking meditation or "walking with awareness." Walking in this way, with great focus, brings the right and left parts of the brain together and increases the interaction and synaptic flow between the two, increasing overall body effectiveness, balance, and healing.

The Etheric Body

The etheric or energetic body is the bioelectric field that surrounds and interpenetrates the whole physical body. Different scientists have called these different things: Wilhelm Reich called it orgone; others have called it vril, or the body field. It is also often called the aura. Cave paintings in Australia that are tens of thousands of years old seem to show auras, as do Christian icons, Hindu murtis, or religious images and countless other paintings and pictures across the world. A few decades ago, Kirilian photography gave us photographic evidence of etheric body, and new devices are being created that actually use this field as a source of power.

The etheric body is both an indicator of "demons" (negative energies, stress, or problems) and a field for target banishing. In other words, a stress or "cut" in the energetic field can indicate a physical issue, and banishing this energetic injury can help the body heal. Likewise, being traumatized through emotional or physical violence can leave a clear impact on the aura, and that trauma can be banished directly by working with the aura as well.

Physically manipulating the aura with other energy fields (such as a person's hand, a magnet, or a TV set) will affect it and thus affect your physical body. Bombarding the aura with a positive energy (chi), such as sunlight or the green energy of nature, is a classic technique for revitalizing the human aura and body, as well as an overall methodology for banishing.

Brain Work

The following exercise, called "Cross Crawl," is taken from the book *Brain Gym* by Paul E. Dennison, Ph.D.

Goal: To banish stress, imbalance, and mental fuzziness.

Procedure: "This exercise helps coordinate right- and left-brain by exercising the information flow between the two hemispheres. It is useful for spelling, writing, listening, reading and comprehension. Stand or sit. Put the right hand across the body to the left knee as you raise it, and then do the same thing for the left hand on the right knee just as if you were marching. Just do this either sitting or standing for about 2 minutes."

Sensory-Overload Banishing

The mental images we bombard our five senses with deeply affect our neurological state of being and this in turn affects our physical health.

Goal: To help you take control of your environment; to help you identify and eliminate sensory stimulants that contribute to the blues, irritation, aches and pains, and stress.

Procedure 1:

1. On a piece of paper write "hear," "smell," "taste," "touch," and "see" as column heads.

2. In each column, note down the typical things that hit your senses over the period of living a normal life for *one day* at work and/or home. What do you eat? What scents do you commonly smell? What do you watch? TV? A computer? How much? What do you touch? What do you listen to?

3. Put a plus sign next to those sensations you think are absolutely positive.

4. Put a minus sign next to those sensations you feel are unpleasant, if only somewhat.

5. Now for the hard part: do your best to either avoid, eliminate, or change all the negatives. Replace them with positive and pleasurable

sensory experiences—music, art, pleasing scents, good and healthy food, calming books, whatever you like.

Procedure 2:

1. Cut off *all* sensory stimulation at home for twenty-four hours. Turn off the radio, TV, computer, washing machine, and telephone—everything. No newspaper, magazines, or books either. Do *nothing* but relax.

2. As the day progresses, examine how you feel. What stresses have gone?

3. Over the following twenty-four hours, slowly reintroduce the sensory stimulants. See which ones make you react really negatively. Eliminate them or limit the time you are exposed to them.

Banishing Coordination and Flow Issues

This simple yoga exercise is designed to increase balance and focus and banish confusion. It may take a number of tries to get that balancing thing down—keep trying!

Goal: To banish stiffness, dizziness, and lack of coordination.

Procedure:

1. Make sure you are barefoot and wearing relaxed clothing.

2. Stand tall, with your arms at your sides. Breathe deeply. Relax.

3. Slowly raise your left leg and place the bottom of the foot on the inside of your right lower thigh, so you are balancing on your right leg. This may take a few tries.

4. Staring straight ahead, raise your arms to the side until they meet, palms together, above your head.

5. Breathe deeply, back straight, and hold the pose as long as you can (ideally a couple of minutes).

6. Slowly lower the left foot and bring your arms back to your sides.

7. Repeat, but this time raise the right leg and balance on the left.

8. When done, relax, meditate on your balance. Relax.

Intentional Walking Banishing

Goal: To exercise; to coordinate the body with the brain and so to banish specific and general health and mind-functioning problems.

Procedure: Wearing comfortable clothes, choose a walking place that is as natural and green as possible. A park is perfect. Do not listen to music, read, eat, or carry a cell phone; all distractions should be avoided.

1. Begin by stretching as you like.

2. After stretching, balance on your left and then right foot, over and over again.

3. Next, raise your right foot off the ground and raise your left arm over your head. Balance in this position for a count of three. Lower your leg and arm. Then switch, raising your left leg and your right arm and balancing for a count of three. Repeat on each side three times.

4. Stop and close your eyes. Meditate for a moment on the center of your being. Depending on your beliefs, this moment may be religious or not. When you feel truly centered, begin to walk.

5. Start with your left foot, if you are right handed; start with the right foot if you are a lefty.

6. Coordinate your breathing with each step. Foot up, breathe in. Foot down, breathe out.

7. Be *aware* of every step. Focus completely on the process of walking. Adjust your stride so that each step you take is the same length and your steps fall at even intervals.

8. Begin to gently swing your hands as you walk. If your right foot is forward, your left arm should swing forward, and vice versa. Now you are using your full mental concentration to coordinate each step, your breath, and your swinging arm. You will go into a meditative state.

9. Keeping your focus, continue walking for at least twenty minutes.

10. When done, repeat the stretching and eyes-closed focusing (steps 2 through 4). Pull all the energy into your center; breathe in and out. Relax.

Note: You can use this procedure to banish a specific problem by visualizing your problem fading into the ground with each step.

Banishing and the Etheric Body

Goal: To clean a person's ethric body, or aura; to banish any negative energy or energetic blockages and so promote specific and general healing.

Procedure: This technique can be done on yourself, but it takes a bit of maneuvering. It is best done on another person. The patient (the person whose aura is being cleared) should wear loose clothing made of natural fibers. The work area should be clean and free of negative influences. (For cleansing ideas for the physical environment, see the Smudging, Aroma Banishing, and Fresh Air Renewal, and the Banishing Wash practices earlier in this chapter.) Both the healer and the patient should be very clean. (See the Magical Bath and Banishing Wash practices for body cleansing ideas.) It is traditional to have a bowl of warm salt water nearby to earth the negative energy being banished.

1. The patient sits in a wooden chair (some say he or she should face north), closes his or her eyes, relaxes, and breathes deeply.

2. The healer washes and dries his or her hands and stands behind the patient.

3. Beginning at the crown of the head, the healer slowly strokes the patient's aura, combing or scraping the energy field to remove any energy blockages, disruptions, and negative energy. (The healer never actually touches the patient.) Both people visualize the dirty aura becoming clean and filled with light as the negative energies are scraped away.

4. The healer slowly works downward, clearing the aura around the entire body until finally reaching the feet. As this process goes on, the healer should periodically clean his or her hands in the bowl of salt water to remove the collected negative energies, then dry the hands and begin again. The healer may do another full session, always beginning at the crown and working down to the feet.

5. When done, dump the water outside, if possible. The patient should wash or shower, if possible, and both the patient and healer should rest for a time.

Note: It is not uncommon for patients to feel real physical changes and even some slight pains during this process. The procedure can be stopped at any time, but often such feelings indicate real banishing changes are happening.

Banishings of the Heart:
Emotional Banishing

So much of what affects us both positively and negatively stems from a triggered emotion or is caused by an emotion. A headache may be caused by an emotionally painful fight with a mate, and, just as often, a headache we have may lead to an argument or fight because we feel terrible. Banishing a negative emotional influence or issue may help you physically, and banishing a negative physical issue or problem will very likely help you in the realm of feelings and emotions.

In this chapter we will look carefully at emotions or feelings to see what the roots of negative emotions are and how they can be banished.

First, you need to acknowledge the power of emotions and feelings in your life, something very difficult for many people to do. Men, especially, are taught to discount or push aside feelings, but all of us avoid uncomfortable or negative feelings that seem to target our sense of self. Some negative feelings, like anger, are often seen as justified. Yet even "righteous anger" (which the Dalai Lama says is like saying "righteous cancer") leaves us drained and feeling irritated, defensive and unhappy. And negative emotions, like anger, seem to be on the rise in our culture.

When you are in the middle of a negative emotion—be it anger, fear, hate, or another—you are blind to its harmful effects on others and on yourself. Looking back, you may think, "What got into me?" And the answer would be: a "demon," an emotional thing that was controlling you, riding you, not vice versa. And your ego is part of the problem. It will justify your anger, hate, or fear, rationalize it, make it worthy of defense.

Encoded in several faiths of the Far East (including Buddhism, Hinduism, and Tantrika) is a concept of the *kleshas*. *Kleshas* translates as "knots" or "aggregates." There are five kleshas, which I see as relating to each of the five elements:

Air   Avidya (ignorance), misconception of our true reality

Fire   Asmita (I-am-ness), defining ourselves by our ego

Water   Raga (attachment), attraction to things that bring us pleasure

Earth   Dvesha (repulsion), aversion to things that bring us pain or discomfort

Spirit   Abhinivesha (clinging to life), fear of death

To achieve growth and liberation, a human being needs to pierce or loosen these emotional knots and so be released from their bondage. In our culture, this means that we need to work through our negative emotional issues and so become free of them. In other words, instead of letting jealousy, anger, and irritation rule our lives, we can choose to bypass or banish those emotional reactions. We do it through the ultimate personal powers of will and love.

You use your will to control your emotional reactions and to change the very basis of these reactions. And you do it out of love for yourself (anger makes you ill, so why inflict that on yourself?), love for the one triggering the emotion ("making" you angry), and love for those who get the blowback of your anger.

You have a choice. With very few exceptions, *you* choose when to feel anger, hate, irritation, guilt, or any other emotional reaction, even though it may not be a conscious choice. You can make a conscious choice to banish these emotional reactions. By banishing the root causes of the negative emotions, banishing the triggers, or even banishing the actual emotion as it floods you, you will become a more balanced and confident person. You will take the reins of your emotional horses in hand and have more control of what does and does not emotionally affect you.

Air: Avidya (Ignorance)

Almost all of the negative reactions we either experience or generate come from ignorance. Ignorance does not mean being stupid, but it does mean being unaware. We are unaware that short-term emotional needs or outbursts have long-term negative impacts and effects that are not obvious at the time. We are unaware of what triggers them. And we are unaware of the root causes for these emotions.

Why are we ignorant or unaware of these things? Mostly because we unconsciously acquired our emotional reactions as we grew up. Traveling through other cultures and even areas of your own country shows you that your emotional reactions are not the only possible ones. Someone from Thailand will not show anger or impatience while in traffic because he or she hasn't learned to, yet a typical American reaction to traffic is impatience, anger, and frustration—a reaction imprinted on us by our parents.

Traffic makes many people irritated, but it doesn't have to. Someone yelling at you makes many people angry, but it doesn't have to.

Yearning for something you can't afford, being jealous of someone who has great things, being deeply hurt by an insult—all of these, our culture tells us, are normal emotional reactions, but they do not have to be.

Let's look at a negative emotion and dissect it. For me, a key one is irritation over not being able to get things done quickly.

What are the destructive effects this emotion will have long-term? Irritation causes me stomach problems, insomnia, and fatigue over the long term. The adrenaline and hyperactivity spurred by my irritation also can spill over into my relationships with my family in a negative way. Once I am in the headspace of being irritated, it is very hard to get out. This state of mind precludes happiness, relaxation, and rest.

Why are these negative emotions triggered? I know from observation that seeing other people working too slowly for my tastes, waiting for what seems an excessive amount of time, feeling overwhelmed by all the tasks I have set myself, all trigger this kind of irritation.

What is the root cause of these emotions? This is often the hardest question to answer. For me, it meant delving into childhood memories. My father was extremely impatient and irritated a lot of the time. Part of this was due to an injury, part was due to alcohol abuse, and part, I'm sure, came from *his* parents. From my mother and school, I consistently got the message that I was capable of more work, higher grades, more tasks. Then I discovered New York City, which was all about speed, efficient use of time, and getting things done. Later on I lived in Tokyo, and it too was all about speed, efficiency, and work.

This carefully thought-out analysis of the roots of this emotion helped me to detach from the triggers and become aware of this emotional reaction, so now I can work to banish it. It is still a work in progress, but I have more control.

Is it easy? No. These old patterns are deeply ingrained, but like everything else, they are transitory and, in a very deep sense, not objectively real. But through your will to be happier and through the love for yourself and others, you can control your emotions in any situation.

Mirroring Anger

Goal: To deflect, calm, and eventually banish the anger of another or your own anger.

Procedure:

1. When you are confronted by someone whose anger is escalating, do not react. Visualize yourself as a mirror—calm, cool, merely reflecting the anger back to the other.

2. Listen to what the person is saying. As his or her anger begins to escalate, begin to talk to them. All your words should be reasonable and not angry; they should not even address the anger. You may say something like, "You seem angry. What can I do to help you with this?" Make sure your tone of voice *exactly* matches the other person's. You will almost hear a click as you match his or her tone.

3. After you link tones, continue talking but slowly lower your voice. The angry person will inevitably also begin to lower his or her voice.

4. Speak lower and lower in tone, saying positive things. Sit down if it is appropriate. The person attacking will either break away and leave or will calm down.

5. Afterwards, see the anger as red energy flow through you both, into the ground.

You can use this technique on yourself using an actual mirror. When you are furious or filled with hate, before dumping it out of yourself, find a mirror (bathrooms are perfect) and imagine that your reflection as the person you hate. Begin your angry rant and slowly lower your tone until the worst of the anger drains away.

Pause, breathe deeply. When ready, confront the object of your anger with calm displeasure. Begin by stating what you're feeling and explaining why.

Teaching and Learning: Unspooling

This procedure banishes the causes of the negative emotions, especially feelings of arrogance or superiority, by finding the root of the emotions and resolving it. It may take a few times, but it can really work!

Goal: To stop emotional outbursts that are triggered unconsciously by banishing the mechanism causing them.

Procedure: First, you must want to change these outbursts and be willing to be honest with yourself. A typical outburst situation might be, for example, patterns of regular road rage or always arguing at a certain holiday time. Often you will have several people saying, tactfully or not, that X "always seems to upset you" or "Why do you get so defensive when people talk about Y?"

1. Next time an unconsciously triggered outburst happens, stop. If someone is helping you with this trigger, have him or her use a key word to alert you when they see this behavior.

2. Freeze the emotion. Be silent. Feel the anger, arrogance, or other upset feeling—whatever it is, really *feel* it.

3. Close your eyes and open your memory, what do you see? When did you feel first this way? Trace your memories of this feeling back in time like a thread. Try to remember all the times you have had this triggered negative feeling. Find the first time that X caused this outburst.

4. *Relive* that first memory. Feel it, taste it, see it.

5. *Resolve* the past memory in your imagination. Defeat the bully, yell back at that brow-beating parent—whatever.

6. When the memory is resolved, in your mind say something like: "It is finished," "I'm done," or "It is resolved."

7. Next time that trigger comes, and you don't react negatively, reward yourself!

The Knowing of Need Banishing

Wanting things is a natural emotional process and a reaction to external stimuli. Yet, to consistently want, want, want, desire, desire, desire, and envy, envy, envy is negative and leads to unhappiness. The key is to knowing the difference between *need* and *want* and to understand how they relate to your life.

Goal: To banish the pain and suffering accompanying excessive desire and envy.

Procedure:

1. At the beginning of each month, take out your checkbook and a small notebook and place them in front of you.

2. In the memo line of one check, write: "My desire." Put the check away in your wallet or pocketbook.

3. Decide what disposable income you have each month. Keep this amount in mind.

4. Say, "I can have what I will if I really will it!"

5. That month, every time you say you want, desire, envy, or need something, write it down in the notebook. If you say out loud that you want it, you can't have it—at least not for a week.

6. If, at the end of a week you still *really need* that thing, buy it with
the designated check. But you can only buy *one* thing you really
want per month.

What will happen is this: you will learn that wants and desires are
ephemeral, transitory, part of the confusion of thoughts and feeling
that swirl through the mind, often influenced by others and the media.
Poof! They are gone in a day or two, unless they are part of a *true*
desire. Waiting a week should let you know.

Note: This banishing is not for things you really need, like food,
rent, practical clothing, and so on. These you buy all month, as you
need. Yet these will not excite you in the same way a desire does.

Banishing the Sorrow Cycle

We all feel sad at times and it is a good and healthy emotion, like all
emotions, when it is appropriate and doesn't consume us. Yet you (or
another) may find yourself stuck in cycles of sadness that are more than
occasional. If you slide into depression, you must seek professional help.
But if you just seem to be sadder than most people or are unable to let
go of a particular sadness, then seek out the root of your tendency toward
sadness and then decide if that is the emotion you want to be feeling.
External events prompt and trigger us, but we always can choose how
we wish to feel. This banishing will allow you to decide whether or not
to be sad and for how long.

Goal: To discover the root stimulus for a cycle of sadness or to understand why you cannot let go of sadness and then banish the root cause.
Procedure:

1. Sit with a pen and paper and some tissues in a quiet, darkened
room. Wear dark colors. Quietly remember the great losses of your

life and the times, from when you were little until now, that you felt deep and truly sad. Let the tears come. Relax into the sorrow. Let it flow over you. Sit in it like in a pool.

2. Write down all the things that come to mind, but do *not* write down the causes of the sorrow. For example, don't write "the death of my cat," but "feeling alone after the loss of Fluffy."

3. After awhile, relax, breathe deeply, and let the sorrow go. Think of the happiest and funniest thing that has happened to you. Try to laugh. Relax.

4. Now look at the paper. Try to find words and ideas that are in common with all your sorrow times. What links them? What triggers this sadness? It may be a feeling of aloneness, abandonment, helplessness, or futility—or maybe something else. It is not uncommon for sorrow patterns to be early established around some perceived guilt.

5. Make a positive affirmation from this feeling. For example: "I forgive myself for not being able to help Fluffy" or "I give myself permission to stop making myself sad over X."

6. Write down a specific positive behavior you will do when you slip into an old sadness pattern. For example: "When I feel so alone, I'll call a friend and go out." Or: "When I feel helpless about suffering, I will send money to a charity."

7. Follow through! Get a friend to help you. The spell or cyclical sadness can be broken by reaching out to friends, to loved ones, to a higher power, to others in need, and so on. Need friends? Follow your interests, help others. *Be* a friend.

Awakening to Feeling Banishing

Sometimes we just shut down emotionally. You may have been so hurt or suffered such a loss that you are just numb. Or maybe you have just given up feeling because you don't like being too vulnerable or sensitive. Maybe you are just going through life, feeling bored and disconnected. In any event, emotions do not go away; they simmer below the surface and, if not expressed, can create some unhealthy complexes and patterns in the unconscious mind that can lead to some bad physical and mental stuff. It may not be completely pleasant to accept and express emotions, but it is who we are as human beings.

Goal: To banish the numbness, emotional boredom, or wall of nonfeeling about you that may have developed.

Procedure:

1. Get a stack of three-by-five index cards, a red pen, and a green pen.

2. On each card write an emotion. Make sure you write both good and bad emotions—happiness, sadness, anger, love, satisfaction, frustration, and so on. Make sure to write emotions that you know or suspect you are blocking or needing.

3. Turn all the cards face down and shuffle them about. Relax. Close your eyes. Concentrate on the image of a beautiful, safe, comfortable place, maybe a beach or field. No one can hurt you here. You are the center of your world. Breathe, relax.

4. Say this affirmation: "I am not my feelings. They are not me. I control what I feel. It doesn't control me."

5. Pick a card. Look at it and open up you heart and mind to that emotion. In your mind, see all the images you associate with that emotion. *Feel* it. Cry, laugh, shout—do whatever feels right.

6. When you become uncomfortable, turn the card over and say, "Stop!" Put it to the side. Close your eyes and return to your beautiful place.

7. Repeat with another card. Say the affirmation, as you need to.

8. Stop when you wish to. Return to the banishing process when you like.

9. End with the affirmation. You have done some intense and powerful work—reward yourself!

Note: Go slow with this banishing. Stick to the positive emotions first. If you feel it is all too much, then seek professional help.

Fire: Asmita (I-am-ness, Ego)

In many ways, the ego is your friend. It gives you a hold on realty, cues you on how to interact with others and with your environment and gives you an identity. Yet emotional problems come when we can see the world only through the ego lens. If you are to banish negative emotions, it is crucial that you realize that there is not objective source for those emotions.

Who are *you*? Are you what you feel? Are you what you think? Are you what you own? Are you your work or what you do for fun or the kid your parents see or your physical body?

No, you are not any of these things. You may think that you are a combination of all these things, but, in the end, you are more than the sum of all these parts. Most religions and spiritual faiths would say that all these things are just a shell or illusions surrounding who you really are—a spiritual being. What you are is beyond all perceptions, ideas, or thoughts.

The being you identify as "me" is merely your view of who you are—and that changes. Added to that is your perception of how others view you, a worker, a father, a lover, a parent, and so on. It helps to think of your "me" as a series of masks, each of which has certain emotional triggers, defaults, and baggage. Think about your emotional states when you are out having fun with your friends as opposed to when you are in school or at work. Your ego has many different sides or facets.

As ever-changing and ever-evolving beings, our sense of self is always in flux. This means our ego is as transitory as everything else in this world is. This knowledge is a great source of freedom and the basis for all successful banishing. Yes, you have patterns, traits, behaviors, and neuroses that you acquired from your environment, but you are not doomed to be stuck with them because there is no fixed *you!*

Banishing the Emotional Blocker: Dropping Defensiveness

A key problem with the ego is the editing of input by emotional rejection. This can result in not hearing or seeing a problem, which in turn leads to lack of communication and the end of many relationships.

Goal: To banish the emotional blocker, even for short periods, in order to help us receive input that is useful—and sometimes vital—to personal growth.

Procedure:

1. Sit down and close your eyes for a time. Have a pad of paper and pen nearby. Visualize the verbal fights and arguments you have had over the last six months or a year. Live through them. Note how you felt during the argument.

2. Now, in short phrases, write on the pad what each argument was about in terms of facts, not feelings.

3. Close your eyes. Run through each fight or argument again, but this time from the point of view of the person you fought against. Act his or her part, *be* that person. See yourself as the bad guy. What are you trying to say? How do you feel?

4. Open your eyes. Next to the argument facts, write down the message you felt the other person was trying to get through to you.

5. Now, under that message, write down a list of behaviors (tone of voice, insulting language, gestures) that make you angry.

6. Make a positive statement about each behavior, such as: "I will not let [list the behavior] blind me to the message."

7. Next time you are in an argument, remember these statements. *Listen.* Ignore the tones, insults, and gestures. What is the *message* being delivered? Often it is very different from the words. For example, your mate nagging you over a chore may really mean "I want attention" or harassing you about you weight issues may mean "I care about you."

8. Respond to the message—and not the emotion—in a positive way. Do not criticize or say "yes, but . . ." or be defensive. See what happens!

"Me, Me, Me" Banishing: The Vision of Humbling

Our ego naturally spins things to empower us. In the mirror, we always look better than in a photo. You see your life as a grand adventure starring you. Things that benefit and praise you are good; things that criticize, hurt, or threaten you are bad. Yet this is a very limiting vision and locks you into a very defined set of thoughts and identities.

Goal: To banish the limited, little-self ego view of the world for a bit and so open your feelings and thoughts to a wider context.

Procedure:

1. Watch or read about the world news.

2. Sit in a quiet place and close your eyes. Visualize yourself in your home, work, at play.

3. See your neighborhood, your town, your county, your country; finally, you are in space looking at the planet earth. Look at all the people, lives, beauty, and horror of our planet.

4. See yourself on the planet, a small part of a vast, interlocking society.

5. Ask yourself, what is my place in my home, my town, my country, the world? How do I affect others? What do I bring to the world? What do I take from the world?

6. From this perspective, looking at the whole planet and all of humanity. How do you feel? What is the point and meaning of your life?

7. Return to your body, but hold the image of the spinning earth in your heart.

8. Next time you feel frustrated or self-centered, close your eyes, think of the world. React with a sense of humbleness, awe, and compassion to minor problems.

"I, Me, Mine": Letting Go of Stuff Banishing

The ego often identifies itself by what it *has*—a job, car, house, big TV, and so on. More, bigger, and better possessions tend to lead to bigger ego. The key truth is that connecting your emotional self to things skews emotional reactions in a negative way.

Goal: To disconnect emotional health from owning stuff; to banish false emotional triggers by banishing unhealthy identification with things.

Procedure:

1. Identify the things in your life that cause arguments, excessive pride, bragging, and bad feeling with others—a new hot car, a great new TV system, a cool computer, a great job, whatever.

2. Close your eyes. See your most favored possessions one at a time.

3. In your mind or out loud say, "Not me." (If you prefer the Hindu meditation, chant *Shruti*, meaning "not this.") Do this for a while until you run out of things that have a hold on you.

4. Later, go and touch each of these things and repeat quietly, "Not me." Each time remember, you are so much more than the things you have. They will someday be dust, but you will live on.

Banishing Emotional Pain

Pain and the fear of pain cause emotional issues. We spend much of our time avoiding emotional hurt. Yet all the emotional strategies we use to avoid pain often end up causing more pain and problems. An easy technique for avoiding emotional pain is to banish the ego pain.

Goal: To banish the cause of emotional pain, even if only temporarily, by banishing the ego pain that happens when confronted by negative emotions.

Procedure:

1. Sit in a quiet place at a restful time. Close your eyes and visualize the last few times you were really hurt or saddened by emotional attacks or criticism, either from others or from yourself.

2. Feel the pain, guilt, disappointment, sadness, anger. Most of all, feel the frustration of the unfairness of it or the inability to do anything about the feelings.

3. Freeze the images in your mind. Pull back. See you and the others as players in a movie or on a screen. That person being criticized or attacked or ignored or whatever is *not* you. It is an *image* of you. This image is what people see, react to, judge, and hurt. The *real* you is above it all, is unknown to others. The real or true you is like a guardian angel, hovering over the argument or fight or problem. So why are you feeling pain? People are merely seeing a mask, a shadow, and a reflection. People often do not truly understand you or really know you, because they are also trapped in seeing what they *think* is you, but that is really only the you that is important in *their* life. Therefore, the emotional thrusts are aimed at a shadow— an image of you. *It isn't meant for the real you!*

4. Next time you are in a situation that is causing you emotional pain, take a deep breath, visualize your *true self* as above you, observing the play. Feel the emotions much as you would when watching a play. Feel sad or sorry or upset for the characters, but remember, the *real* you is not playing this game. When the show is over, it is over.

Banishing the Masks and Finding the Wellspring

Deep down, you know your ego is just a series of personas or masks you show to the world, but sometimes, because of these different masks, you get confused as to what you are feeling and why. The problem is discovering your *real* feelings about something, the true feelings that transcend situation.

Goal: To banish ego masks and so discover (or rediscover) the wellspring or root of your *true* feelings that are not part from the ever-changing emotional responses of the ego.

Procedure:

1. In a semidark room, get into a relaxed and quiet seated position.

2. Look at yourself in a mirror. Who are you?

3. Think of each of your roles in life. They might be something like: son/daughter, parent, worker, lover, entertainer, partyer, sports player, political activist, traveler, and so on.

4. Think about the last time you were angry and the last time you were really happy. Think about the situations and causes of each of these feelings.

5. Now slowly go through each of your ego-masks again and ask, "How would the parent me feel about this? The worker? The lover? The political activist? The partyer?" Soon you will encounter confusion because, of course, the point of view (mask) and the situation often changes the emotional reaction.

6. Close your eyes. Think about this.

7. Again visualize in the mirror each of your ego masks. To each one say, "I am more than a [name the mask]."

8. Finally, look again in the mirror. You are *you*—beyond roles, beyond situations, beyond the push and pull of duties, traditions, responsibilities, and programming.

9. Think again about the things that caused anger and happiness. How does the *real* you feel above these things now? It is likely you will feel calm, maybe slightly one way or the other, but not pulled. This is your true, calm center. Next time you are in an emotional whirlwind, take a moment to pull back from all your masks and be here.

Water: Raga (Attachment)

We are trapped in a two-sided cycle of negative emotions when we consistently attach our sense of pleasure and well-being to transitory sensations, objects, or people. Being dependent on another person for your happiness is neurotic. We call such people "dependent" in a negative sense. If you feel good because you have a new car, then the car breaks down, is it any surprise that the resulting emotion is pain, anger, or frustration—or all three? We are unhappy, so we go shopping and soon feel better. But then the pleasure fades, and the original cause of the need for pleasure (a miserable relationship, a bad job) remains.

Or we may want to attach ourselves to another person, go shopping, or buy that new car to bring ourselves pleasure, but it never lasts. Then, later, we are unhappy and jealous of others who have the mate, car, or things we don't. We also may be frustrated and resentful. Things change. Such pleasures, being external, are transitory.

Does this mean you can't enjoy pleasure or do things that you like to do for fun and enjoyment? No, of course not. These things are not in and of themselves bad, but they trap you in emotional yo-yo patterns that drive you crazy if you let them. The key problem is *attachment* to those things and to the pleasure they momentarily generate. Pleasure is always fleeting and does not always lead to happiness.

The first step to detaching is to ask: "How can I emotionally let go of X when I don't get it or if I lose it?"

By accepting the fact that you will not get everything you desire and that even the things you do get are transitory, including all relationships, you can begin the work of detaching from the emotional strings that pull you like a puppet. Once you have found a place of detachment, then you can selectively banish those emotions and reactions that push and pull you like storm waves. Once you get the knack of detaching, a whole new level of satisfaction and happiness will become apparent to you, and, through awareness and conscious banishing of negative attachments and emotions, you will become freer than before.

Detaching does not mean being passive or ceasing to strive for things, but it means keeping a realistic view of what you need and what you will to be connected to as opposed to unhealthy attachments and unrealistic emotional expectations. It also means accepting other people and their irrational attachments and emotional responses without allowing them to hook you into creating negative emotional states of your own.

In this section we examine emotions or feelings and see what the roots of negative emotions are and how they can be banished in theory, yet to begin this process you first need to acknowledge the power of emotions and feelings in your life and to realize that the root problem is that we are bombarded with and sometimes manipulated by these emotions. Often it may be that feelings themselves are more addictive and crazy making than what supposedly causes those feelings; lover, friend, car, or whatever.

Letting Go of the Brambles Banishing

Holding on to emotional pain causes heartache and sometimes trauma. In romance, it is not the friendly breakups we remember or obsess over—it is the horrible ones. We usually don't obsess over leaving a job voluntarily as much as getting fired.

Goal: To dissolve our attachment to painful or traumatic emotional experiences, to banish them from our mental tape loops and dreams.

Procedure:

1. Find *all* physical traces of the pain-causing person or situation, no matter how small, and throw them out. Even e-mail and documents should be deleted—and deleted from the deleted items file! When you are done, *nothing* should exist that even remotely reminds you of the situation, person, or pain.

2. Now, in a calm place and time, eyes closed, visualize this: you are holding a thorn-covered branch, a bramble. It hurts; it causes pain and agony. Your hand is bleeding.

   This bramble is the painful person/situation. Name it as such. Curse it! It is old and tired and dead, but still you hang on to it. You have tried to let go, your hand begins to heal, but then you grip it again. Again you feel pain, again you bleed.

4. Breathe deeply. Silently forgive yourself. If the bramble is a single person, forgive him or her; if it's a situation, forgive everyone involved. Forgiveness is the price you must pay to let go.

5. Breathe deeply again and feel the pain leave you with each deep breath.

6. Slowly let go of the bramble. See it fall to the ground. Slowly it sinks into the ground and becomes part of the earth. See your hand heal, the blood disappear. The pain is gone.

7. Smile. It is time to move on. You have awoken from a bad dream.

8. Get up, go out, and have fun!

   Note: Repeat if necessary.

Letting Go of Worry Banishing

Worry is an epidemic; our culture sends so much frightening information at us from so many different angles that we are like emotional ping-pong balls. Worry causes stress and leads, if excessive, to a host of physical and mental problems.

   Goal: To banish excessive and intense worrying when it serves no purpose.

Procedure:

1. Severely limit your exposure to alarmist media, especially news. Allow yourself only one shot of news a day—one paper, one TV newscast, whatever.

2. Limit your intense worrying to three things at a time:

- One thing about the world (for example, global warming)

- One thing about your loved ones (rising health-care costs)

- One thing about yourself (excess weight)

3. Do something about each worry. For example, write a letter, make a call, or join a group that is working to halt global warming. Call, write, or e-mail your politicians about your concern with rising health-care costs. Look into other health-care programs; join one of many groups working on this issue. Exercise at least once a day; make a healthier eating list and follow it.

   The key is ignoring free-floating worry and anxiety by focusing on, say, three concerns, then actually doing something about them. Anyone can do something about even the largest worry issues, such as unemployment, war, and poverty, step by step. Positive action banishes worry!

Letting Go of People and Relationship Banishing

Sometimes a relationship is simply over. If it is with a person, maybe they have moved on, left, passed on, or simply don't want anything to do with you. You also might have a passionate relationship with a career, an addiction, or a home or place, but that relationship is over. Now *you* must make a clean break and banish your attachment to that person or thing.

Goal: To end an intense emotional attachment; to banish a fixation or tape loops that won't let you move on.

Procedure:

1. With pen, paper, glue, crayons, magazine pictures, photos, and so on, make a collage about the person or thing you want to banish from your life. Take your time doing it. Make sure you include all the good and bad things about the relationship in image form. Make it complete. Review and relive all your feelings; the good, the bad, the pleasurable, the painful. All emotions should come to the fore. The collage may end up with many layers! Invest time and emotion into it.

2. When you are done, prop up the collage. Talk to it, meditate on it. Obsess on it. Apologize, rage, cry, yell at it!

3. When you are completely finished with it, emotionally, take it outside in the middle of the night and burn it. As it burns, say good-bye. The relationship is over, it is gone, it is finished finally. You are letting go—you are free.

4. Gather the ashes and put them in a small box.

5. If you follow a particular religious faith or have an emotional connection with the idea, take the box to a cemetery or other sacred area. In an appropriate manner, bury it discreetly on the edges of such a place, maybe in the bushes or woods, making sure you do not disturb the graves or visitors. Do so with a brief silent prayer and lay it to rest. If you aren't religious or funeral customs have no emotional impact for you, then simply bury it somewhere. Say a final good-bye. Thank the person or thing for a valuable learning experience. Move on.

Transforming Grief Banishing

Grief is a fact of life. Often the cause of our continual sorrow is empathy for a damaged person or a place that is suffering. We must learn to live with this sorrow and make something positive from it.

Goal: To banish the worst aspects of grief so as to make it bearable.
Procedure:

1. Set aside a small corner or part of a shelf for a memory spot. If you are religious, think of it as a small altar. Have there a candle and a picture of the person or pet or place that is afflicted. Light a candle.

2. If you are religious, pray at this spot for relief from suffering. If you are not religious, visualize relief coming to the afflicted and to you.

3. Breathe deeply, see the sorrow enter the candle flame, see the flame enter your heart.

4. Feel the sorrow in your heart turn to caring, to love, to compassion.

5. Feel the compassion fill your body, emanate from your body, fill the room, and flow into the image before you.

6. Blow out the candle. Either pray or visualize peace for all involved.
   Repeat this practice as necessary. Use this memory spot for as long as you feel the need to. Whenever you feel sorrow overwhelming you, close your eyes and transform it into compassion and love. If the object of your compassion is alive, make sure you tell them you love them and are thinking of them.

Risking Emotions: Banishing Fear of Feeling

You may be emotionally shut down for any number of reasons. Shock, trauma, emotional abuse or betrayal, maybe feeling too much just seems to get you hurt all the time. Somewhere and sometime you decided to avoid complicated emotions and emotional involvements. You may avoid meeting people, getting a dog, committing to a relationship, all because you fear getting hurt. Removing the false security of the idea that no feelings = no pain allows you to experience the joys and the sorrows of emotional involvement with perspective.

Goal: To instill emotional self-confidence and remove the fear of feeling.

Practice:

1. Find a place that is really isolated. It could be way out in the woods or in a basement room, as long as it is far from people or pretty soundproof!

2. Wearing comfortable clothes, go to this place. Sit quietly and visualize all the emotional chaos that led you to shutting down. Remember what anger feels like.

3. Now, stand up and *scream!* Yell! Hit the air, ground, anything! Feel anger, rage, hate—let it out! Scream at the top of your lungs!!!!

4. When exhausted, sit down. Remember happiness, fun, love!

5. Now stand up again and *laugh!* Get hysterical! Crack up! Hug yourself, trees, anything!

6. When exhausted, sit down. Remember sadness, sorrow, and pain of loss.

7. Now, stand and *cry!* Wail! Beat the ground, sob, curl in a ball— feel it!

8. When exhausted, sit down. Remember love, kindness, caring, infatuations, Mother/Father/Sister love, hot romantic love, friendship/pals love.

9. Now, stand up and *sing!* Sing silly love songs, sing anything, make sounds, howl, bark, whistle, feel your heart overflowing with love, love, love!

10. When you are exhausted, sit and be quiet. Think of nothing. Feel yourself. How are you? Love yourself for wanting to feel, for being brave enough to open up.

11. If you need a final affirmation before you leave, sing the Beatles' song "All You Need Is Love." Then go out and love someone!

Earth: Dvesha (Repulsion)

Just as attachment leads to unhappiness, disappointment, and negative feelings, so too does repulsion. Those things you hate, despise, and are repelled by are just as firmly rooted in your mind, heart, and life and cause just as many problems as the things you lust after, desire, and want.

In the same way that attachment is a double bind, so too is repulsion. If you fear, hate, or loathe something, then you avoid dealing with it. As the time approaches when you have to deal with it—or you *might* have to deal with it—the negative emotions intensify. Then, when and if the actual event occurs, you have a let down. You are filled with self-loathing and self-criticism because of all the unnecessary fear and worry you invested. If the resolution or confrontation doesn't come, you are simply left with more fear, worry, and dread because there has been no closure. The anticipation of a negative event or situation often generates far more anxiety and emotional turmoil (repulsion) than the actual situation itself.

For example, I often dreaded going to the dentist. Days before a session, I began to have feelings of dread, worry, and fear. I dealt with days of these feelings, then the actual visit was usually not more than an hour. And as I made my appointment for my next filling, the cycle started all over again. This cycle of fear, repulsion, confrontation, and dealing with it seemed so natural that it was easy not to question it.

Repulsion and all the negative feelings surrounding it never really die down or get resolved because they are self-perpetuating. If we are not worried about X, then we fear and dread Y; if one irrational fear doesn't come true, there are plenty more where that came from.

The old adage "what you fear most will come true" is rather depressing and pessimistic, but there is a kernel of validity in it. Whatever you put tremendous focus and will into is bound to manifest because you are telling the universe that you have a need—a need to confront some issue or thing or event that is stuck in your craw. This is why hypochondriacs get really sick eventually, and people who fear spiders always seem to run into them. Part of us wants to be repulsed—we often get the same sort of thrill from it as being attached. Just look at the popularity of thrillers and horror movies whose sole purpose is to make you uncomfortable, fearful, and repelled!

Yet constant stress, worry, hate, repulsion, and fear poison us. They wear down the immune system and lead to a host of mental and physical problems.

The key is to recognize that you are in control of your emotional responses, including repulsion, fear, and hate. The place to begin is to stop, get centered, clear and ask yourself three questions:

1. What do I *really* hate or fear here?

2. What is the root cause of this repulsion?

3. Will this repulsion help me in any way, or can I let it go?

Once you get clear on the answers to some or all of these questions, then you can banish that repulsion.

To give you an example, I am repulsed by heights, and I fear high places like observation platforms and cliffs. For years I avoided such places and will admit to still occasionally avoiding them. But I am over the worst of my fear and rarely think about this repulsion. My answers to the questions were:

1. I hate and fear heights, but, looking closer, not all of them. I'm fine in a 747, but freak looking down from a fifty-story building. It was a sense of vertigo, of deep-seated disorientation. My fear was instinctual, but also illogical and irrational, and I acknowledged it as such.

2. After lots of reflection, I remembered some very scary falls I had as a kid, including one from the roof. So I'm quite sure that the root cause of my fear was some sort of trauma, though I don't remember it clearly.

3. I intellectually knew that the fear I have about heights was not helping me, but the worry seemed a part of me. Even my friends considered it part of my personality. But some experiences caused me to shift my point of view, to challenge the belief that this was an inevitable repulsion that I had to adapt to. It was *not* something I was born with; it was acquired and so could be changed.

Once I realized that my fear could be banished, I decided to confront and deal with it in such a way that I could become detached, or at least more neutral, about heights. I got a pal to teach me how to rappel down cliffs! The first time was, of course, the hardest. I did meditations, repeated affirmations, and did it. After a number of times, I got pretty good at it. It never ever became comfortable, but the repulsion became manageable. Looking back, the fear seemed irrational, and I couldn't comprehend what I'd been making such a fuss over.

By banishing those emotional knee-jerk responses of repulsion or attachment we get some breathing room to become aware of these reactions and decide what our will is in each situation. We can cease to let external things manipulate us by banishing the feelings of fear, loathing, and hate that keep us connected to them.

Accepting and Transforming Phobias Banishing

We all have things, people, and situations we're instinctively repelled by. Some are repelled by spiders, others by loud people. Avoiding some things (like spiders) can be fine, but if you want to banish certain irrational fears or phobias, you can.

Goal: To banish and/or at least become neutral concerning certain fears, phobias, or instant dislikes.

Procedure:

1. Target the fear, hatred, or phobia you want to banish. Write it down on a piece of paper in a clear statement. For example, "I will to banish my extreme fear of snakes" or "I will to banish my extreme dislike of short people."

2. Sit quietly in a calm place; close your eyes and visualize the first time you had this fear. Dig deep in your memory. Did you have a bad experience as a child with a snake? Did a parent drill into you a prejudice towards short people? Take your time, try to remember, and relive the initial fear or hate fixated on this thing.

3. If you can't remember the origin, remember and relive the first time you can clearly remember feeling the hate or fear towards that fixation. Feel it deeply. *Be* there. When you are completely immersed in the feeling, clearly say your "I will to banish" statement. Repeat it several times while letting the feeling slip through you and vanish.

3. Next, go online and fine pictures of the object of your phobia. Print out a dozen or so, the more repelling the better.

4. For at least one week, every day, at a time of quiet, take out these photos. Repeat the "I will to banish" statement. Study

each photo carefully for thirty seconds. Relive the initial fear or anger. Say, "It has no hold on me." Let the feeling fade away, repeat with the next photo.

5. When you can do this exercise and remain emotionally neutral, destroy the photos while repeating, "It has no hold on me."

6. Finally, find the real thing. Go find a snake and handle it; go hang out with short people. Do this for a short time. Repeat silently to yourself "It has no hold on me." If you begin to feel anger or fear, then stop. Try again another time.

You will find, if you are truly focused, that the knee-jerk fear or hate is banished quickly, but a lesser emotional unease or dislike takes much longer to banish. Keep up the process until you feel as emotionally balanced as you would like to be.

Accepting and Not Reacting: Banishing Hooks

The heart of most feelings of repulsion lie within how we truly feel about ourselves. One of the truest aphorisms is "we dislike in others what we dislike about ourselves." Often-lazy people complain about how lazy other people are; the angriest drivers hate other aggressive drivers and so on. Accepting yourself, flaws and all, often banishes your negative feelings toward others and helps you to accept others.

Goal: To banish negative feelings, complaining, and irritation by discovering what behaviors in others repel you and how they manifest in your behaviors.

Procedure: It is useful to have a friend or loved one help with this process initially. The other option is to keep a very accurate journal for a week.

1. Your pal (or you in your journal) needs to note down everything that really irritates you over the period of a week. Every complaint and expressions of irritation, anger, dislike, and so on needs to be noted.

2. Next, look at them all. You will usually find several themes; note them down. For example, you might find most of your complaining has to do with rudeness, people who lie, sloppy eaters, or lazy workers. Write these key irritants on a piece of paper.

3. At a calm, relaxed time, take this paper and look in a mirror. Turn each statement into a question for yourself. For example, "Am I ever rude?"

4. Answer yourself truthfully, maybe saying something like, "Sometimes I am rude, but I don't mean to be."

5. Then say, "I accept this about myself and so accept this in others." Truly accept this.

6. Breathe deeply. Visualize the last time someone was rude to you. Let it go. Forgive that person, or at least be neutral. It is *not* your problem.

7. Move to the next item. Repeat the exact same process.

8. The next time someone is rude to you (or whatever the irritation is), *let it go*. It isn't your problem. Then say, "I accept this about myself and so accept this in others."

Note: Accepting is *not* liking nor is it endorsing. It is simply being neutral, not letting it hook or emotionally hurt you.

Banishing Fear

Fear is the root of all negative emotions, including arrogance, bigotry, and hate. We fear losing something; anger is caused by fear of hurt or pain. Fear shuts us down emotionally and fills us with a paralyzing dread. Fear is a natural reaction that keeps us safe as a species, yet today so many messages of fear are beaming at us that we can become almost consumed by it. While this banishing will not eliminate all fear in your life, it can help.

Goal: To banish the immediate paralysis and toxic upset caused by an immediate fear situation; to banish and release the fear before it is converted into anger or another negative projection.

Procedure: Practice this process *before* something scary happens to you.

1. Accept the fear; say, "I am scared." Even if it seems silly to be scared, the emotion is real.

2. Identify the fear. Is it fear for your safety or for another's safety? A vague fear (of something such as terrorism) or an immediate fear (a weaving driver)? State out loud what you're afraid of.

3. If the fear persists, visualize the fear as a dark cloud covering you. Note your physical reactions (heart pounding, sweating, whatever).

4. Visualize the fear cloud passing through you. It fills you, but it passes through you, it is behind you. It is gone. Breathe deeply. The fear passes. Breathe deeply. The fear is passing. Breathe deeply; the fear is going. It is replaced by worry.

5. Act. Calmly act. Move into the other lane, call 911, bandage the cut, or accept that there are terrorists out there but not here and now in your room.

6. If the fear is not immediate, decide where the fear came from. The TV news? A rumor? A nightmare? Try to avoid and eliminate such needless causes of fear, especially if they cause panic.

Note: If panic attacks continue, seek a professional for help. This exercise is very helpful and becomes more effective with practice.

Walking Through and Banishing Nightmares

Everyone has woken up in a state of fear at one point or another. Often these nightmare moments can offer you a great opportunity to deal directly with a root fear in the unconscious. Banishing the monsters in a dream can have a liberating affect on your waking life.

Goal: To confront and deal directly with a manifestation of an unconscious repulsion.

Procedure: If you have a recurring nightmare (of a vampire, of falling, of a murderer chasing you, whatever) then adjust your preparations.

1. If you are religious, decide what the most powerful word or phrase is in your belief system. If you are Catholic, for example, it may be a phrase used to exorcise "demons." Buddhists may use a seed syllable (like *phat!*, the lightning bolt).

2. Think also of a gesture or movement used to cast out evil. It may be making the sign of the cross or a special mudra (gesture), such as the sword mudra.

3. If you are not religious (or even if you are, but you want to deal more in "action"), decide what kind of weapon you would be most comfortable with—even if you have never touched one in your life. For example, mine was a classic .45 automatic with a religious symbol on the handle. Others prefer swords or knives.

If your fear is of something abstract like falling, try a rope or a pair of wings.

4. Spend several hours visualizing this weapon. *See* it, *feel* it, *know* it.

5. As you slip into sleep, practice your religious banishing phrase and gesture or clearly visualize your weapon in your hand.

6. When confronted by the "demon" (the thing you fear—the vampire monster, the murderer), do not run. Confront it! Then either banish it with your phrase and gesture (put all your will into it) or kill it with your weapon.

    This may take a few tries. If you can't banish it in one dream, switch to another weapon. Do you need holy water? A flamethrower? It is up to you. It is a dream so anything is possible! The key is to take the offensive.

Note: Often when you awake from a successful shot at this banishing, you will envision some immediate practical ways to change your life. Your unconscious is teaching or telling you something. Listen!

Banishing Guilt

Guilt is a pretty common issue for many people. Your family, culture, religious tradition, and so on have likely taught you that it is okay to feel certain feelings and want to do certain things, but not okay to feel other feelings or do other things. But feelings and desires are not rational; they exist in their own plane and are quite complex. Often we can trace feelings or desires to a specific experience, but they also may simply be a natural part of our being. Excessive or misplaced guilt about these feelings or desires can be really damaging and negative and thus should be banished.

Goal: To accept your feelings and to banish harmful guilt over feeling what you feel or wanting what you want.

Procedure:

1. On a piece of paper, after much thinking and visualizing, list the specific feelings you have that cause you excessive guilt or that make you ashamed. These are often of a sexual or lustful nature, or they are secret hates and irritations.

2. One by one, immerse yourself in these feelings. As you begin to feel guilt or shame, clearly say: "I can feel what I feel. My heart is mine. I can let go of harmful feelings. I can cherish positive feelings. My heart is true."

3. Let your guilt, shame, or discomfort fade away. Note that nothing happened. No one was hurt. No sin was committed. It was only a feeling, it didn't cause harm, even if it was negative! *Feeling* is not the same as *doing*.

4. Forgive yourself. Use whatever words you need. If you are religious, ask divinity for forgiveness. Accept that forgiveness.

5. Continue the process. Repeat as necessary.

Note: Some emotions may cause you some real pain, and you should work to banish or work through these if they negatively impact your life or the lives of others. It may be that you need to express these openly with a therapist to get some peace. You will know. Other negative emotions we feel inside are part of life. Accept them, don't suppress them or always act upon them, but allow yourself, in the privacy of your own inner mind, the ability to feel things you wouldn't express publicly. These feelings are normal—we all have a shadow side.

Spirit: Abhinivesha (Clinging to Life)

All organisms, from protozoa to humans, are instinctively driven by the urge to survive. A fear of death is so pervasive in our mind, body, and heart that we scarcely notice it except in times of threat or intense stress. Yet this fear of death "demon"strates the ultimate attachment. The urge to survive, no matter what, usually trumps almost all other urges in the human experience, except for the key one: love.

True love can override the survival mechanism; the "higher power" of such love causes parents to sacrifice for children, lovers to give up their lives for their loved ones, and comrades to sacrifice their lives for their fellows. We all recognize the heroism and purity of such love and, deep down, wonder if we could do the same if such a dire situation was presented to us. Those who are able to make this ultimate sacrifice have managed to pierce this klesha, to bypass the hardwired biological survival instinct with a higher purpose, what could be called true will through love.

All strong fears are rooted in the fear of death, of losing our ego, of losing our attachments to the things and people we love. Unless we confront and let go of our strongest fears, they control us. If you will to do this, then you need to trace the root of those fears (fear of being fired, fear of being homeless, fear of rejection) to the real source of all fear: the fear of personal extinction. If you can accept your own eventual demise and, in doing so largely banish, your fear of it, then the influence of all other fears on your life fades.

Working on minimizing an unhealthy fear of death does not mean you should want to die or that you will not do what you can to survive; a healthy desire to live is normal. It does mean acknowledging and accepting your own ending as *you*. When you do this, the obsessive clinging to life cannot control or warp you any more; it cannot generate and support other fears. All fears become easier to banish once the big fear is dealt with. Accepting that you will die eventually, and that fact is neither good nor bad, frees up a lot of positive energy.

Banishing the Fear of Death

Many of our negative feelings can be traced to a fear of death and dying. Everyone should, of course, love life and live to the fullest, but that also means accepting that the end of life is a given. Western culture has made a point of removing death from everyday life. Death is something to fight, ignore, put off. Yet death does not have to be the horror our culture assumes it is.

Goal: To banish the boogeyman view of death and replace it with a healthier and more emotionally positive view.

Procedure:

1. Sit quietly and close your eyes. Maybe face north, the traditional direction of death. Remember your earliest image of death and all the times you have been confronted with its reality. Remember funerals, grieving, and so on.

2. Next, visualize death itself. Many fall back on the typical image of death as a black robed skeleton with a scythe. Concentrate on this image. Is Death male or female or neither? Let the image evolve and change, as it wants.

3. When you have a clear image of a personified Death, give it wings—large, beautiful, glorious wings. Realize that Death is an angel. In Judeo-Christian culture, it is the angel Azrael. Other cultures have different names. Ask Death its name or name it yourself.

4. In your mind, talk to Death. Get angry, sad, furious, resigned. Tell Death your feelings, how upset you are by what he/she has

done, how afraid you are of him/her. Strongly express all your feelings.

5. Now listen. Does Death have a message for you? Is Death showing you any symbols or images? Think about them.

6. When the conversation is done, forgive Death. Accept his/her existence as necessary. Thank Death for granting some understanding. If you are religious, accept Death as a part of the divine, maybe as an angel (messenger) of the divine.

7. Finish by bidding Death to depart, asking him/her to interact with you in this positive form from now on. Chat with Death again whenever you wish.

Note: If at any point during this visualization exercise you get spooked or feel fear, stop it. If you are religious, pray or call upon the divine as white light to banish the fear. Either try again at a later time or skip this banishing.

The Acceptance of Ending Banishing

People often do very irrational things and express very irrational feelings when thinking about their eventual end, especially as they get older. Understanding, truly understanding, that your time on this earth is limited is a powerful knowledge. Our culture does amazing things to avoid this understanding, often focusing on youth culture and stopping aging and simply excluding older people from the media spotlight. The fact is, we will all die, and for the majority of us, we don't know when. Accepting your ending frees you to begin many things and gives positive context to your works. This banishing is appropriate at any time in your life when you are thinking on your life and maybe avoiding thinking about its end—after a friend's funeral, after a disaster, maybe after a near brush with death.

Goal: To banish self-centered feelings and fixations and to focus on the "great work" of our lives by accepting our eventual ending.

Procedure: This visualization should be done in a natural setting, if possible, while watching a setting sun.

1. Visualize yourself as the sun. You are a star, unique, like none other. Think of all the learning you have. Think of all the skills and experiences you have. Think of all the work you have done, the things you have made, the relationships you have had.

2. Close your eyes. Imagine if you died right now, right as the sun sets. Imagine your death as a stone dropped in a quiet pond. The stone (you) is gone, but the ripples carry on and on. How has your life affected the world you left behind?

3. Visualize your whole life, from beginning to end. As you look at your finished life, ask yourself these questions:

    What did I do that brought positive feelings to others?
    What did I do that will last in some form or another?
    What did I do that has improved this world?
    What did I not do that I wish I had done?
    What did I begin but leave unfinished?

4. Open your eyes to the sunset. It is the most beautiful sunset you have ever seen. You are alive. You can do anything, change any attitude, help others, help the world, leave some real good behind. Someday, maybe soon, maybe a long way off, you will end. What do you want your life to mean? Think, plan, act— now. Go and do good.

Centering in the Now: Banishing Overload

This is a good banishing to do when you feel overloaded, overwhelmed, or inundated with the chaos of life. If you are feeling swept along in your life flood, pause and do this procedure to center, detach from life for a bit, and banish your feeling of lack of control.

Goal: To banish illusions, confusion, overload, and lack of control that hinder true emotions and actions.

Procedure: Do this wherever you like, but in a place where you can close your eyes safely: sitting on a bus, sitting at work, resting on the couch, or quietly sitting alone on a bench.

1. Close your eyes. Imagine that suddenly time *stops*. Everyone is frozen. All sound, all motion, all living, all action—stopped. Only you are free. Time and energy and matter are with you, but all else is dead, still, frozen.

2. Breathe deeply. Relax. Laugh! You are utterly free from the stresses and craziness of your daily life. It is all halted. You have a breathing space! Collect your thoughts, fantasize, stretch, meditate, whistle—do what you like. You are outside time.

3. Now you are in control. You will decide how your life goes; you are in control of your feelings, emotions, and reactions. You just needed a time out to remember this.

4. When ready, open your eyes; start the clock again. Life goes whirling along, but you have a newly refreshed calm center. You have banished the false feeling that you are not in control. You are *always* the center of your life.

   (By the way, laughter is *always* a powerful banisher!)

Banishing Lack of Closure

Much of our clinging to and obsession with life, and thus our fear and dislike of death, has to do with anger and sorrow over deaths we have dealt with in the past. Yet cultures around the world banish the negative onus surrounding death through a clear process of emotional closure. They focus on the love that transcends death and time. This love is always alive.

Goal: To mitigate or banish, through love and remembrance, a lack of closure due to unrequited sorrow and fear surrounding the death of loved ones.

Procedure:

1. Find a small corner of your home that will serve as an ancestor niche or shrine. It might be a small shelf, or, if you like to keep it private, a closeable cupboard or cabinet.

2. Find or copy pictures of all the loved ones you have lost to death. Pets, friends, and revered leaders who you didn't personally know can be included. You may also have small mementos, souvenirs, and so on associated with these people. On a piece of board or in a picture frame, arrange all of these pictures and items. As you create this collage, name each of your loved ones. Remind yourself of all the love you feel for them and of all the love they gave to and still awake in you.

3. When you are done, clean the shrine area and place other things in it, as you like—flowers, a small bowl of sweets, a small thimble from Grandma Smith, whatever makes you feel good.

4. When you are done, bless this shrine. If you are religious, use the prayers or chants of your faith. If you aren't, write a poem

of love and connectedness for all those you love who have died. Read it with great feeling.

5. Sit and quietly visualize all these loved ones around you, comforting you, helping and loving you. Whether you believe in life after death or not, these people loved you and still love you. Love never dies. You still love them, and that love is here and now and real. Let that love heal and nourish and help you.

6. Finish as you like, return when you want, love as you will.

Banishing Fear of the Great Transformation

Many poets have seen death as the Great Opportunity or, as several have said, "the beginning of the Great Adventure!" Cultivating this attitude is the ultimate banishing of negative death feelings and ends a morbid attachment and clinging to this life.

Goal: To banish your fear of death; to help you accept death as not an end but as a transformation.

Procedure:

1. Go to a graveyard (any kind will do) and find a nice quiet spot. Sit on a bench. Choose a nice, sunny day with few people around.

2. Sit quietly and simply be. Breathe the fresh air, hear the birds, and look at the flowers, trees, and green growing plants. Really, graveyards are places filled with life and living things.

3. Think on this phrase and then say it, realizing its truth: "Neither matter nor energy can be destroyed: matter transforms into energy, energy transforms into matter." In other words, physics shows us a key truth: nothing truly ends. Realize that life is energy; it cannot cease to exist. It merely changes form.

4. Look at the graves of all the dead people around you. Their bodies transforming into the grass and trees. Their energy is gone, but still exists in a different form. Imagine all the forms this energy could be in. Angels? Other living beings? The sun, wind, and rain? Maybe it exists as other energy, maybe as matter, for one changes into the other and both are closer to identical than most want to admit. One thing we know: nothing ceases to exist. Whether you have a religious belief in an afterlife or not, hold this in your mind. Only appearances change; the basic reality (energy and matter) is eternal.

5. All things change all the time, no matter how you feel about it! Embrace this truth and banish the pain caused by attachment to the illusion of permanence. In fact, the dance of change is beautiful and brings us most of the joys of life. Live in joy.

Banishings of the Mind:
Psychological and Thought Processes

Banishing thoughts, patterns, attitudes, ways of approaching things, beliefs, and all intellectually dysfunctional or negative processes is a tricky business. In many ways, the head rules all. The brain is the command center for head, heart, and body, and it is here that the real work of any sort of banishing is done.

Like the body and the heart, the mind can be lazy, indolent, misused, ignored, or simply turned over to someone else. This book is not for people who simply let others do their thinking for them. The ability to banish something in and via the mind requires an ability to step back from your own thoughts, ideas, and mental behaviors and admit that some things are simply not working for you and need to be changed. This is far easier to say than to do. We can vow to stop a negative behavior, but actually getting the mind to shift is far harder.

The oft-repeated line "it is all in your mind" is actually quite true. This author assumes that there is no one objective reality. Reality is really what you perceive it to be, and this perception, in turn, affects you emotionally and physically. We are participants in the manifestation of reality, not simply players on a stage that is set before us.

Yet the way we live our lives is based on the understanding that we share a world—that your house, street, job, and so on exist and you maneuver amongst all of life's rich variables interacting with all of them as best you can. It is a mental map we acquire as we grow up and which is set by our culture. Unfortunately, this map is the racetrack of the ego. Your ego is in control of this reality framework because it is based on survival patterns set tens of thousands of years ago.

Many people are quite fine with this whole reality construction until some part of it does not function the way they (or their ego) thinks it should. Losing a job, losing a loved one, dealing with stresses that seem unwarranted or undeserved, tend to shatter your whole world because your world is created from a very delicate map that you work very hard to create and follow. At these times of dissatisfaction, stress, and problems we often turn to spiritual help—forces outside of our mental universe.

Yet turning to spirit leads often to three choices. First, spiritual help can tell us, "Here is the real reality as laid down by X in this book (or other dogma). Follow it and all will be well." And this works for some people. But it means turning over your Will, your ability to use your mind, to another authority.

Or spiritual succor may simply say, "Accept it all. This is the way it is. Learn to live with it. It is God's will." In this case, the original problems, pain, and issues that need resolution are still there and still negative. So coping strategies—escapism, self-medication, and so on— are brought into play.

The third choice is a looking inward, believing that the source of spirit is, in fact, the mind. Not the ego, not the brain, and all those electrical impulses, but the Mind. This Mind transcends the reality map of our thinking self. If we can pull back from our Mind to a place beyond our intellect, we can banish and change our thinking and the problems generated in our mind.

To banish neurotic thought patterns, unwarranted beliefs, harmful ideas or worries, or mental attachments, you first need to be able to grasp them, understand them, and have power over them. You have to distance yourself from them and their causes. You must be able to say, "That is a dysfunctional and negative thought pattern. It is not *me* because my thinking processes are not me. I am above and beyond these processes, and therefore can change them if I will to do so with love."

This chapter is about banishing small to medium-sized mental "demons." Mental "demons" are often more pernicious and deeper than other types. Some require lots of banishing, but others just require a belief that there are alternative ways of thinking and then acting on them. Some issues, like serious depression, may require professional help because the roots may be biological or may be so overwhelming that your will may simply need support and guidance. In fact, sometimes simply reaching out to others for help *is* the banishing required.

As we enter the realm of the mind and the possibilities of mental banishing, the different banishings will be focused on the key components of Ego, Superego, Id, Subconscious, and Self and the powers behind them, of which there are five:

1. to know

2. to will

3. to dare

4. to keep silent, and

5. to *be*

These powers are nothing more than modes of behavior that you can adopt and that will lead you to control over your Mind. The potential is there, as shown by the four traditional powers, but it is the fifth power, the power of being, that shows what is at the core of it all. When you hold these keys in your hand, then you will have the Knowledge, the Will, the ability to Dare, and the keen focus (silence) to Banish the negative from the center of your being, and so become more Aware.

Air: to Know

Here we are talking about intellectual knowledge, thinking, conscious behavior. The traditional psychological label for this mind state is *ego,* the sense of a *me* at the center of all learning, knowing, and giving information. You were born into a reality that has set schemas, or ways of seeing and making sense of the world, including beliefs, traditions, social norms and mores, rules, relationships, accepted sources of information, and so on. While all human beings in the world are essentially the same, these social and cultural schemas set us clearly and sometimes violently apart.

Each of us believes that our schema—our way of knowing—and our sources of authoritative knowledge are the correct ones. Even if you are more globally informed and are as open–minded as can be, and work very hard at accepting that a variety of worldviews, traditions, and beliefs are equally valid, deep down, other schemas are not naturally *your* schemas because you were born and educated and exist in *your* culture.

Different people from different reality maps don't just think differently, they also learn differently. And how they learn is influenced not just by their schemas and natal reality framework, but also by their innate personalities. Thus, knowing and learning are very individual processes. You know things based on your prior schemas and on how you learn.

For many, knowledge is seen as a finished or completed unit of information, labeled "real" and then cemented in the mind. These building blocks are then linked together through your schema via your ego and expressed as either fact or opinion. If someone disagrees with your opinion, then they clearly don't grasp the "truth" and are wrong.

The whole knowledge acquisition system is guided by the ego, which is programmed to see itself as the center of all things. This system assumes that when you learn something, the process of acquiring knowledge is over. But something can be proven bedrock truth one day can be proven later to be quite false. In fact, truth is relative to each culture, religion, political party, shift in scientific paradigms, and so on. Most of what we "know" are facts that are determined as true by someone else. Some (the world is round) fit our basic scientific schema because we simply accept that others have proven. Other so-called facts (*this* holy book holds God's law, there are no ghosts) are actually quite debatable and fall under the rubric of beliefs.

You get your knowledge from three basic places:

1. *The schema that forms your worldview or view of reality.* You often do not question such knowledge, and it is usually so deeply rooted in your childhood as to be unconscious.

2. *Other people or sources.* These range from well-studied teachers, texts, and experts to idiots on the radio or TV. All of this "knowledge," unless tested and proven, is *not* authoritative. Usually these streams of information are delivered with the goal of not only informing you but also bending your view and schema for a specific end.

3. *Direct experience of your outer or inner reality through your perceptions.* This includes things like how an apple tastes and what is called apperceiving, or directly experiencing, the essence of something, like "knowing" that you have a soul.

All three modes of acquiring knowledge hinge on number three, because all the information thrown at you goes through your filter, your ability to perceive. By banishing blockages or limitations on your "reality funnel," you can change amazing amounts of ideas, patterns, and thought processes. You can take back control of your learning from those sources of information that seek to control your mind. By banishing knowledge-based—and ego-based—false attitudes, opinions and certainties, you are open to ways of thinking and solutions that were not apparent. You can also banish tape loops of negative knowledge that cause needless harm and have no basis in truth.

Much of this banishing work is done through guided internal, or open, meditation. Observing *how* you think and learn, then using the powers of your mind to puzzle out what the blockages are and free yourself from the self-imposed walls is an incredibly liberating experience. By retaining and reclaiming mental flexibility through knowledge, you are open to the universe.

Banish Compulsive Thoughts

Goal: To examine your thought process and discover the root of unhealthy or unhappy compulsive thought streams and banish them.
Procedure:

1. Sit in a quiet place and meditate. Make sure you will not be interrupted for a while and that nothing is pressing at the moment. Close your eyes, relax, and breathe deeply.

2. When you are calm, pull back from your thoughts and observe them. Let your thoughts just drift in and out of your mind. They will arise spontaneously: doing laundry, work tasks, a shopping list, thoughts about family, strange images from movies and TV, and so on. Let them drift.

3. As they arise, do not attach to them or follow them. For example, if your thought is, "Oh, I have to make dinner tonight," do not follow it with, "What shall I make? Pasta sounds good. Okay,

I'll need sauce and I'd better go to the store. Oh, I'll have to get salad, too. That reminds me. . . ."

When you catch yourself following a line of thought, *stop*. Begin observing again.

4. As you observe your thoughts flow by, observe your emotional reactions to them. What thoughts trigger anxiety? Anger? Sadness? Where are these thoughts coming from?

5. Find one thought that keeps repeating, that keeps coming back, and is *now* triggering a bad feeling. Stop that thought. Examine it. *Trace it back.*

   For example, maybe the thought of shopping causes anxiety. Stop. Why does this thought bother you? When did you associate anxiety with shopping? Trace the thought-emotional links back, like a chain.

   It is likely that one thought will lead back to another, then to another, and so on.

6. When you have reached a place where you feel the anxiety comes from, breathe deeply in and out. Let the anxiety flow down and out of you. Meditate on this thought. Relax. Keep focused on it until it no longer bothers you. Let it go.

Slowing Down: Banishing Hyperthought

The hyper pace of incoming data, media, and so on has speeded up in our culture to such a degree that people are in constant anxiety just trying to stay on top of everything they think and do.

Goal: To slow down your mind and sanely process ideas, tasks, and thoughts so as not to simply react to things without being fully aware; to stop your mind from racing.

Procedure:

1. When feeling overwhelmed, like your head is going to burst, sit in a quiet place. Relax. Breathe deeply. Be comfortable. Make sure you are not disturbed.

2. Withdraw from the chaos of your mind a bit. Observe your thoughts. Do not try and control them, do not focus on any of them. Do not get hooked into following any of the thoughts. If that happens, stop and begin again. Simply watch your thoughts flow by, like they are racing by on a movie screen.

3. Breathe deeply. Slow your breath down. Relax. As your breathing and heart slow, so will the flow of your thoughts.

4. Count your thoughts. For example, "Oh, I was late to that meeting!" (1) "My foot itches." (2) "I hope it is sunny tomorrow." (3) That is all. Just count them. When you reach 100, stop.

5. Now let a thought come. Hold it. Examine it. Deal with it. You have banished that overrun and overwhelmed feeling. You have control of your mind, not the other way around.

Mental Ruts Banishing Meditation

One of the hardest things to do is to get perspective, to get out of mental ruts, to break a cycle of repetitive thinking and feeling and doing that you know is not good but is hard to get out of.

Goal: To banish a negative mental box, rut, or cycle you want to be rid of.

Procedure:

1. Sit quietly and meditate without distractions or interruptions. Relax, breathe deeply, and unwind.

2. Choose a persona or character to be your mental observer. It can be an animal, a famous person, anything you like. (I use a monkey.) Visualize it clearly and see it sitting to the side.

3. Now *become* the observer. You are not you—now you are whatever you have chosen. You have no feelings or thoughts. You simply observe, like a camera.

4. Look at that other person's life (your life). See yourself getting up, getting ready, going to work, shopping, dealing with family, and going to bed. Observe the last full day of your life from beginning to end *without making judgments or reacting*.

5. Observe the negative behaviors, the things that make that person unhappy or stressed. How could this person stop these painful situations? What thoughts or reactions led up to these problems? How could things be done differently? What could be avoided?

6. When you like, finish your meditation. Dissolve the observer in your mind. Breathe deeply. Come back to your mind.

7. Note down all the advice your observer can give you about changing the way you think and act.

Negative Thinking Banishing

Thoughts are negative when they evoke negative feelings and even negative physical reactions. Identifying these thoughts and their source gives you a means to redirect or banish them.

Goal: To first identify, then imagine, and finally banish thoughts or thought complexes that are harmful to you.

Procedure:

1. Sit in quiet meditation, breathing deeply, relaxed, uninterrupted. Let your thoughts flow; do not attach to any of them.

2. Eventually, the thought or thought complex troubling you will arise. Let it go. It will eventually arise again, let it go.

3. Finally it will insistently arise again. This time hold it. Push away all other thoughts and focus on that one thought, anxiety, worry, or fear.

4. Holding this thought, breathe deeply. Keep your focus on the thought but examine your feelings. What emotions do you feel? Fear? Horror? Worry? How do you physically feel? Are you hot? Is your stomach upset? Thoroughly examine these feelings.

5. Keeping the harmful thought in focus, relax your body—your arms, legs, stomach, and so on.

6. Relax your feelings. Let the fear flow away, the worry fade. Focus on *only* the feelings until they are neutral.

7. Now examine your negative thought. It has lost its power over you. *In itself* it is not evil or scary or repulsive. It merely is.

8. Let the thought fade away. See it burn, sink into water, blow as dust in the air, or be buried in the earth. It is gone. If it returns, it will be powerless to hurt you or compel you.

9. Repeat this procedure as necessary.

Banishing Away Anxiety Meditation

Our thoughts can rush us into a state of panic or anxiety as conceptions and memories push all sorts of buttons. This exercise will stop the overload process and bring you back to a calm place.

Goal: To stop a mental anxiety meltdown and bring a calm, steadying focus back to your life by banishing the panic.

Procedure:

1. When confronting a situation that slams you with panic, first, *stop.* Do not react. Breathe deeply, slowly. Do not shout, speak, or say anything.

2. Stand up straight (you will likely be hunched over) and balance yourself. Make sure your feet are on the ground. Focus on your physical balance.

3. Smile—even if you don't feel like it. Force yourself to smile.

4. Withdraw from the thought process. Let the flood to thoughts flow by. Similarly, let the flood of emotions flow through and out of you.

5. Find the center of your being, in your heart region. Focus on that. Breathe deeply.

6. Sit down. Be calm. Relax. You are fine.

7. Close your eyes, visualize yourself as a rock in a river. It flows around you. You are calm, steady, not moving. You are clear.

8. In your mind, *one thought at a time,* review the mental calming steps you just followed.

    Now:

9. Decide on a course of action, *one thought at a time.* Do *not* dwell on feelings that arise; they flow away. You are a rock.

10. Deal with the panic-causing situation in a sane and calm manner.

Fire: to Will

Here we will be looking at behavioral and mental modification, changing patterns. The traditional psychological label for the will is superego, the "big parent" part of the mind that is formed from traditions, accepted rules, norms and all other solidified authoritative elements acting as a part of our Mind.

By discovering and adhering as close as possible to what it is you really want, you become a happier, better-adjusted whole person, and thus fall into step with your "True Will," i.e.: what you are on this earth to do. By getting clear in how you think, what your thought patterns are, and on how to identify positive and negative thought patterns, you can then Banish these negative patterns, sloppy thinking, and wasted fantasies that make you unhappy.

Your True Will (capital T, capital W) is your life path, your higher purpose, or what you are on this planet to do. Your will (lower case w) is the strength of your character forged in the fires of experience and the struggles of survival. The latter is held by the superego most of the time. It is really all about your persona of yourself as the boss, the top-dog mask of intent that you present to the world. Call it the internal extension of your higher identity, your charisma, or force of personality that you use to get what you want or need through plans and patterns of thought. We are talking about what is often termed the "force of will."

This superego persona should not be confused with your True Will, that inner voice of your Self or higher consciousness that guides you into doing what is right and true. Terrible dictators and bigots often mistake their force of will for some sort of divine True Will. On a lesser scale, you may have firsthand experience with petty tyrants, abusive people, overbearing bosses, and charismatic but twisted religious figures, all imposing their ideas on others. If this physical world is all there is, each of us contesting the world via our force of will, then the constant, primate push and shove of politics, religious conflicts, and the belief that "might makes right" is easily explained.

Yet a majority of people know that there is more than just this endless sparring of superego-driven personality conflicts. By stepping back and looking at this play of will in your world and in yourself, then you can make changes; you can banish the unwanted infliction of such forces on you or your world, and you can alter the way your own force of will projects from you.

This control is key, because it is through your will that your thoughts, ideas, and visions are put into practice as a mental plan that you then feel free to follow. Although this system originally evolved thousands of years ago to help us get the things we needed to survive, the same set of impulses now often goes awry because they are directed at things the will decides are needs when, in fact, they are merely want, whims.

The superego helps you survive by telling you what is right, what is wrong, how to behave, and what rules you must follow in order to live properly. Yet overuse of this component makes you too aggressive, overbearing, dominating, overburdened, guilty, overly responsible, and burned out. A necessary balance can be achieved by banishing excessive use of this faculty.

If you seem to be not getting the things you strive for, if your relationships seem to be suffering from your overactive demands, or if you seem to be pushing away people, things, employment, success, your will is out of balance. You are trying to force things that cannot be forced. If you are constantly feeling guilty, unworthy, and that you are always wrong, or if have a nagging parent voice in your head dominating and harassing you, you need to banish that superego "demon."

Removing such imbalance and impediments will allow the True Will or higher Self to naturally deliver to you what you need. It allows love to flow, internally and externally, and opposition often will dissolve.

The force of your personality driven by your perceived (thought out) wants and desires sets up many conscious patterns in how you think, how you view the universe, and how you perceive and plan out action steps to survive and prosper. In Japan, the overriding schemas for such patterns of personal will centered on concepts like harmony and cooperation with the clan. In the United States, the overriding schema for the use of will is competition—competition for jobs, mates, food, and success on all levels. Examination of these acquired general and specific thought patterns of interaction help give you a handle on why you think the way you do and maybe how to banish those patterns that are harming you.

While these patterns are difficult to banish, it is possible to do so with some True Will and love. We can use contemplative or analytical meditation, sometimes called heart yoga, in which empathy for others and yourself is brought into the thinking and will process using visualization exercises, projection techniques, mental reprogramming exercises, and with improved thought organization.

Banishing Confusion and Fuzzy Thinking

There are times when you just don't seem to be thinking right, when mental confusion fills you, when you are distracted by everything. A simple exercise will help you center and stay focused, banishing the fuzzies and the lack of an anchor.

Goal: To refocus thinking, banish the chaotic distractions swamping your mind, and get your mind back on track by being the boss of your own mental processes.

Procedure: When you feel the need to mentally reboot and refocus, find a place free if interruptions and distractions. Outside, in nature, is better, but anyplace with fresh air is okay.

1. Stretch your whole body while leaning gently left, right, back, and forward. Be sure to stretch your toes.

2. Stand with your feet a comfortable distance apart and your knees bent slightly.

3. Focus your mental energy on your third eye. Focus on a simple image of a ball of light. Still your mind, think only on this ball. Keep your focus on it until you see the ball of light clearly.

4. While looking straight ahead, bring your hands together, cupping them toward each other without touching, in front of your chest. See the ball of light there between your cupped, parallel hands.

5. Holding the ball of light, move your hands in front of your belly while still standing straight.

6. Slowly move your hands and the ball of light up your body to your forehead/third eye. Inhale deeply as you do so and let the light pervade your mind.

7. Move the ball of light and your hands back down to your belly as you exhale.

8. Repeat this process three times or more.

9. At the last inhalation, release the ball of light. It fills your mind with energy and clarity.

10. Relax. Get to work!

Banishing the Overmonitor

As we speak to others, write to others, love and have fun with others, there is a little part of us that watches and corrects. When things are balanced, your little inner monitor does a good job making sure you don't insult people, sound silly, or make atrocious mistakes. Yet sometimes that monitor is so busy correcting you thoughts, words, and actions that you fear to do what you want because you might make a mistake.

Goal: To banish overmonitoring and obsessive self-correcting and self-critiquing.

Procedure:

1. Get a piece of paper and a pen. Sit in a place where you will not be disturbed. Relax, breathe deeply.

2. In the paper, intentionally misspell several words. For example, "hapy."

3. Write several completely untrue statements, like "I'm president of the USA."

4. Write several nasty statements you normally would never say— "I hate puppies and eat them for dinner!"

5. Now close your eyes. Relax. Breathe deeply. Find the tugging, nagging source of thoughts filling you. Find the *urge* to correct these statements.

6. Breathe in and out, focusing on this urge until you have a hold on it. Push all feelings to the side. Visualize it as a thing or symbol or person, as you like. This is your monitor.

7. Focus your will on it. Shrink it! Make it smaller! It will protest, try to escape. Hold it!

8. Dominate and command it; tell it exactly what you want it to do. Tell it: "I have control over you. You exist to help me, not punish me. You only have the power to edit what I will you to edit!"

9. Now release it. It bows and obeys you.

10. Relax, breathe deeply. Open your eyes.

11. Next time you feel bullied by your monitor, visualize the symbol or image of your monitor and tell it to back off! Make all the mistakes you want.

Banishing Self-Hate Meditation

We often have a little voice in our head that criticizes us, tells us how bad we are, and bosses us around. Called the superego, it really echoes the voices of our parents and other adults who told us as kids what was right and wrong, and so on. As we grow up, this inner parent can cause all sorts of problems, guilt, neuroses, and so on.

Goal: To banish the affects of self-hate in our minds or at least banish its most harmful effects.

Procedure: Find a picture of yourself as a toddler or child. Take it to a place where you can sit comfortably and not be interrupted.

1. Breathe deeply, relax, and let your mind flow. Meditate on the picture of your young self.

2. Remember the times you were yelled at, bothered, punished, and so on. Feel the feelings of unfairness fill you.

3. See yourself as that child, but now you are growing, growing, growing. You are a giant. You tower over the people who yelled at you and punished you.

4. Yell back at them! Defend yourself! Tell them what you think! Unleash all those words you were afraid to say before! See the grownups cower. They are asking you to forgive them!

5. Relax, breathe deeply. Forgive them. Tell them you forgive them.

6. Ask them to forgive you. They do. You embrace.

7. Let the image fade. In your mind hold three thoughts, in succession:

> *I forgive all adults who hurt me or made me feel guilty.*
> *I am forgiven by all who punished me for anything I may have done.*
> *I forgive myself, love myself, and am a worthwhile person who deserves love.*

8. Finish your meditation as you wish.

9. Keep the picture of yourself as a child to remember that you *are* still a worthwhile person who is deserving of love, and you always will be.

Banishing Obstacles to True Will Meditation

Often our feelings of unhappiness, dissatisfaction, and depression do not have a single source or cause. Sometimes it may be hard to pin down exactly why you are unhappy or what is the cause. It may be that the reason is bigger than this or that, it may be a question of your life orbit, your path.

Goal: To banish unhappiness by correcting the orbit of your life.

Procedure:

1. Sit quietly and close your eyes. See yourself as a blazing star in space, slowly moving in your own specific orbit. Look back and see where you have been in your life. See the successful moments, accomplishments, and relationships as points along your orbital path. See all the "wrong" moments—failed relationships, bad jobs,

and fish-out-of-water experiences as moments that pulled you off this orbit you made through space.

2. Think carefully. What do the "on orbit" experiences and relationships have in common? What sorts of things got you off track and made you unhappy?

3. Where are you now? Are you right on track with your orbit? Slightly off? Way off?

4. Project the orbit into the future from the past positive experiences you had. Where will your orbit take you? Is this the right orbit for you?

No one can tell you where you have been or where you are meant to go. But I know this for sure: every man and every woman is a star. Each star has an optimal orbit that it needs to follow to be all that it can be, to make the most of this life, and to do what it needs to do to fulfill its part of the larger divine pattern.

Many forces about us, including other people, institutions, and negative traditions will try their best, for their own reasons, to pull stars off their orbits, to snare them, and to enslave them to their will. Commit now to seeking real happiness through doing your own True Will—that is, following the path that is right for *you*, regardless of what others say or do.

Most people who are basically unhappy, who are mean or unkind, who self-medicate themselves are simply not doing their True Will. These people have been convinced by society and the people around them that they need to do X, Y, or Z, that this is the way to live and that they should therefore be happy. But they are not and therefore assume that something is wrong with them that needs medication or something else that is missing.

5. The primary reality check you have is your inner voice. Listen to that quiet voice of truth within you now.

Remember, it is *now* that matters most. Your ego (and others) will try and convince you that you can put off doing your true will until you have done X, Y, or Z. *Now* is what counts. Make a plan to change your life *now,* to avoid (and banish) those people or influences that are holding you back, and to do *your* True Will!

Bad Attitude Banishing

This quick vibration banishing is excellent for banishing bad attitudes. Deeper problems may not fly away with this procedure, but sometimes we just need a quick "snap out if it!" to banish that dark mental cloud.

Goal: To jolt your current mental mindset out of a negative groove and into a positive one.

Procedure: Do this in a place where you can chant fairly loud and no one will call the police or worry about your sanity.

1. Stand up and stretch. Relax, breathe deeply, and become calm, even if you are in a rotten mood.

2. Face the east. Think of where you want to be mentally and decide on a word for it, such as *positive, chipper, happy,* or *accepting.*

3. Take a deep breath and chant the word. It should vibrate your whole body (think of Gregorian chants or the hum of a massage machine). Chant the word several times, stretching the word out to last at least ten seconds.

4. Chant the word three more times, focusing the first vibration on your head, the second on your heart, the third on your lower body.

5. Chant it one more time for as long as possible.

6. Sit, breathe, and empty your mind. Relax.

7. Say "I am [chanted word]." And so you are.

Water: to Dare

The traditional psychological label for this power to dare is id, the primitive instinctual, "animal" part of our Mind that supplies us with primate drives, compulsions, and instinctual focus, what's sometimes called the "Dragon Mind" or reptilian mind. This is the area where our deep intuitive drives live, the "beast" part of the inner mind. It is a remnant of your gestation to a fully human. When you were growing from a single cell to a baby in your mother's womb, you went through all the evolutionary stages, from amphibian to reptile to mammal to human being, and all these stages still exist in your body and your mind. The lower-thought level, your animal nature, is still embodied in your lower cortex and comprises a key part of your mind.

The id comprises the sexual drive to mate and reproduce, the fight-or-flight drive that assures survival, and all those primal aggressive or submissive tendencies that we see in animals every day. It also is the deep-seated primal source of pleasure and the drive to actually do things that our Will plans to do.

The id is explosive, and our culture, for a large part, suppresses these drives to such an extent that negative patterns of thinking and doing are obvious every day. Outbursts of anger and bullying in the workplace, date rape, and road rage are all examples of the reptilian mind running amok. When we turn control of our mind over to the id, then only the ego and superego determine what happens, thus creating the dog-eat-dog mode of existence. Mob violence is a perfect example of animal nature being given full-rein with the blessing of our ego and will. Perpetrators may not plan a massacre, but their id unleashes the power to act on pure aggressiveness.

Yet we do not want to banish the id completely. It can be—and needs to be—a powerful and forceful ally. While overly restricting these primal and seemingly uncontrollable urges can cause all kinds of mental and even physical problems, accepting them and channeling their volcanic powers appropriately through the balancing and banishing of internal blockages can unleash tremendous personal power and lead us too a much happier and fulfilling existence. The key is balance and controlling when and how to let the beast out.

The first step is acknowledging the id and accepting—and loving—that animal side to your mind. This means accepting that you have a powerful and real sex drive, that you have the very real potential to aggressiveness (especially when it comes to self-defense), and that you have desires, fantasies, and primal thoughts and drives that are not conscious, but can be glimpsed in art, dreams, and sometimes actions that are not consciously explainable.

The next step is to realize that negative expressions of this id harms you and others. The ego will cover up and explain away these negatives as being acceptable when they are not. The will to do something can be a terrible thing if empowered with an unleashed id, as every "insane" dictator has shown us over the years.

The final step is to become aware of how and when it functions in you life. A perfect example is the tantrum. The mental process of a tantrum looks like this: someone does something you don't like or won't give you something you want. You get pissed off, irritated, and then just flip out irrationally. If you were to analyze this tantrum, you might say it feels like being possessed. When we use comments like "he was out of his mind" or "he lost it," we are talking about the id taking possession of the conscious mind.

Once you are clear on the mental processes and mental and emotional triggers that give the id a free pass to wreck havoc, then you can banish those mental dams, barriers, compulsions, and weaknesses that let the beast loose unsupervised.

Id-related banishing is done through physical and mental coordination on a higher level, often called active meditation. When barriers to the id leave you with little drive or motivation, banishing takes the form of motivating exercises, unblocking activities, and work that stimulates action.

By linking your instinctual drives to your will, you can make things happen. By acknowledging your primal drives and using them in a coordinated effort with other parts of your mind, you can banish the "demons" of jealousy, sloth, indecision, and passivity to accomplish amazing things.

Banishing Apathy and Boredom

The urge to wildness and chaos is the root of the mental power of the id. It is the force of unreason, of breaking taboos, and so on. It has great power because it connects directly with the primitive level of instincts. When you feel jaded, bored, apathetic, and unmotivated with your life, let the id power shake it up and banish these things!

Goal: To shake yourself up and banish boredom, apathy, and unmotivated attitudes.

Procedure: Take a day off for a trip into wilderness. The place you go must be deep woods, mountains, empty beach, or desert. It must be truly wild and warm. You must be completely alone and in a place where you won't be interrupted.

1. Pack: a bottle of wine (if you drink), other intoxicants of your choice, your favorite rich and delicious food (even if you are on a

diet), something to use for beating a rhythm (such as a small drum or rhythm sticks), and a blanket.

2. Go to your wild place. Lay out the blanket, and then take off all your clothes.

3. Drink your wine, eat your food, explore your area—all completely naked. (If the weather is too chilly, go home and do this exercise another day.)

4. When you are a little high and have eaten, call to the wild spirit within you and in this wilderness. For example, you might say, "Wild wood spirit come to me! Wild spirit in my heart set me free! I am wild and joyful, so may it be!" Be spontaneous and wild!

5. Pound the drum or beat the rhythm sticks (or use whatever other rhythm-making instruments you've brought) and dance! Completely go wild, abandon all shyness, and inhibition! Let fly! Spontaneously sing and banish all the dull, soulless, gray stuff from your life. This is *life!* Freedom! Joy!

6. When you are done, collapse laughing!

7. Meditate, make love to yourself, explore, sing—do whatever the wild spirit moves you to do next. Do *not* write, read, and think about work or home responsibilities.

8. Offer some food and wine to the wild spirit of the place and inside you, if you like.

9. In the late afternoon, when you come down and you are safe to drive, go home. Don't tell anyone what you did.

10. Notice how you feel and act the next few days. Repeat as necessary.

Banishing Mental Limitations

Many speak of thinking outside the box, but few really know how to banish this set of limitations, if only for a little while. Sometimes you just need a push. Here is one technique.

Goal: To radically shift mental perspectives and so banish mental limitations, stale thinking patterns, and the mental boxes we've created.

Procedure: You will change your head space by taking on a new role, one that is utterly different from who you are. The role playing is temporary and internal. Whatever new point of view you plan to adopt, assume it for a full day.

1. Choose one of the following scenarios or create your own—as long as it is outlandish and impossible!

- Aliens have taken over everyone on the planet except you. You have to pretend to be absolutely normal in your work or life, or they will catch on to you. How will you deal with them? How will you discover what they really want? How will you do things differently?

- You have been chosen by the universe as "the Most Important Person." Everything you say and do today will be carefully observed by a vast audience of adoring fans in a secret universe. Be a good role model for them! It isn't what you do, but how you do it!

- You are a secret agent, a hero who has saved the world at least a dozen times, but today you are undercover. You have to go about your normal day but you are always alert for the secret codes and information in everything. Who are your secret enemies? Allies? It is impossible to know, but it is all very exciting. In the end, of course, you will save the world.

2. After living one of these wild fantasies for one full day, sit and smile and review the day. How did you view things differently? What

amused you the most? How did it change your way of thinking or acting? What can you bring from this day into your normal day to open up your world a bit? What other wild scenarios could you use to jolt you out of your specific rut?

Banishing Sex Blocks and Body Armor

Countless researchers and psychiatrists have written books on the crucial links between sex and neuroses, physical problems, and so on. Most of these issues have to do, obviously, with lack of sex or with repressed sexuality or sexual guilt. One little banishing ritual will not solve such intense issues, of course, but simply opening up more sexually will "break up body armor," as Wilhelm Reich said. This body armor, he claims, leads to all sorts of mental and even physical problems.

Goal: To increase sexual activity and focus this releasing of energies on banishing rigidity and body armor, which in turn can help banish all sorts of other problems.

Procedure: A few preparatory hints:

- This banishing should be done solo. Making love with another person is an intimate and powerful form of sharing, but banishing is about eliminating, not joining.

- My doctor (a regular M.D.) says you should have an orgasm once every two or three days. Orgasms help your overall body by lowering and relieving tension, stress, and muscular rigidity—all things that can lead to health problems. For men, orgasms especially help your prostate as you get older.

- Sexual banishing is about self-love (masturbation). Privacy, relaxation, and comfort are crucial.

- To use sexual banishing, initiate self-love exactly when you feel the least sexually interested—after a horrible day at work, after a terrible fight, when you are terribly sad about a loss, or anytime you are completely tense and stressed out.

1. Take a shower and relax a bit.

2. Create a positive, attractive setting. Light candles or incense. Bring in flowers.

3. Using whatever toys or lubricants you love and using whatever visual stimuli or fantasies you like, initiate self-love. It may take some effort if you are really angry, sad, or upset. But persevere. You control your mind and thus your sexuality (which is all in your mind).

4. When you approach orgasm, use whatever words or thoughts you need to focus on in order to let go of the *negative stuff*.

5. Afterwards, relax. Do not jump up and do something. Enjoy your relaxation. Remember: being relaxed is normal; being stressed, tense, and unhappy is not. Breathe deeply. Feel all your muscles and bones relax. The tension sinks into the ground and is replaced with warmth and security.

6. Meditate for at least ten minutes.

Banishing Procrastination

One of the most pervasive and pernicious mental "demons," as I'm sure you will agree, is procrastination. You get overwhelmed, tired, and burned out, and then come the dreaded words, "I'll do it later." Procrastination is a mental issue, and shifting your mind a bit can help banish the "demon."

Goal: To jolt your mind out of lazy, in-your-head procrastination patterns so you actually do what you think of doing.

Procedure: First buy some treats that you love but are normally forbidden (chocolate works well for so many people). Get a small notebook that is just for projects. Keep it on you.

1. Sit quietly in a relaxing space where you will not be disturbed. Breathe deeply and relax. Let your mind drift. Do not hold onto any thoughts; let them go by.

2. What nagging thoughts keep bothering you? Many of them are about things to do. Which ones are things you have put off, that you need to do but haven't?

3. Breathe deeply. Notice and remember the mental energy and stress these undone, but should-be-done things drain from you.

4. Decide, firmly, to free up this wasted stress and transform it into positive action.

5. In your mind, see a list of three things you have put off.

6. Breathe deeply, come out of your meditation, and write those three things in your notebook.

7. Without waiting, do the first thing on your list. Every excuse in the world will come to you—every possible distraction. Punch through them! Banish them! Do your task!

8. When you are done, have your treat.

Make sure that each day you accomplish one thing on your list. *Always* reward yourself with a treat when you are done. Keep your list of things to do current. Try to get into the habit of doing a chore right when you think of it. Repeat the above meditation once a month or so if you are a chronic procrastinator.

Banishing Self-Defeating Mind Games

We often are our own worst enemy and critic. You, like most everybody else, likely say negative things about yourself every day without noticing: "I'm so dumb!" "What an idiot I am!" "I can't do anything right!" Sound familiar? This constant negative mental programming can and should be stopped. It leads to all kinds of negative mindsets and harms self-esteem.

Goal: To banish negative mental mind games and self-defeating thought loops.

Procedure:

1. Note on a piece of paper all the common self-critical, self-negative things you commonly say, even when you don't notice. It is helpful to have a friend help with this list, since many of the things you say are unconscious.

2. Meditate in a calm, relaxed manner without being disturbed. Breathe deeply and relax. Let your mind become quiet.

3. After a few minutes, open your eyes. Read the first negative statement. Then refute it. For example, if your first statement is "Oh, I'm so dumb," you might reply, "No, I'm not dumb. I make mistakes, but I am a smart person!"

4. Stop. Close your eyes. Recognize the truth of this positive statement.

5. Move to the next negative statement and refute it. Do the same for all the statements on your list.

6. Run through the whole list three times.

7. When you are done, physically cross out each negative statement and write the positive statement next to it.

8. Keep this paper in your wallet. If you start to slide into self-criticism (have a friend watch you), do the meditation again. Remember, we are all human. We are not perfect. We make and learn from mistakes, but we need self-confidence to improve.

Earth: to Keep Silent

The traditional psychological label for this part of consciousness is the unconscious, that vast ocean or "deep mind" upon which rests the conscious mind. Your unconscious mind is a mysterious place of symbols, images, strange dialogues, and your own private myths. Rarely linear or straightforward, the nature of your unconscious mind and the communication it has with your aware or conscious mind is something psychologists and mystics have debated about for centuries. Any therapist, psychologist, psychiatrist, or other mental health worker will attest to the effect that unconscious stresses and complexes can have on a person's body, heart, and mind.

The key to truly finding the roots of deep, painful issues is looking at the unconscious mind. Maybe they were caused by traumas in the long forgotten past; maybe they have to do with unresolved issues of sexuality or self-image. How do we deal directly with the unconscious mind in terms of banishing? The answer is radical but simple: we have to bypass our conscious mind and our ego and go directly to the source with an open heart and mind.

The cognitive process we usually use to understand things does not apply to the unconscious mind. Instead, we can either listen carefully to the unconscious mind to hear what it wills to tell us, or we can plant seeds of banishing in the unconscious mind through means that bypass the ego guardian. Both processes are done with the same focus as the other kinds of banishing, but with much more finesse and a lot more openness to what the results will be.

Dreams are one way the unconscious mind both processes and delivers hints on what is cooking in its deep recesses. Weird dreams about being at work or school or being embarrassed are your unconscious mind's way of dealing with stresses and fears from your normal life. There are also dreams that seem to have intense significance, but whose symbols are puzzling at the same time. Pay attention to your dreams, especially the latter type, especially if you are focusing on something that needs to be banished. Your unconscious mind is trying to give you a key to unlock that door you are thinking of.

There are ways to petition your deep, unconscious mind and ways to plant specific requests in it through images, actions, and rituals. We can use rituals, or sequences of action that are symbolic, to alter unconscious patterns and so affect the conscious world. These rituals can include working with dreams, sigils, artwork, and deep mediation.

You may find that something you wish to banish has deeper and more complex roots than you realize. If that is the case, seeking professional help, therapy, and medication is always a banishing option.

Dream Work Banishing Technique

You may have a particular worry, fear, traumatic event, or obsession that you know will bother your sleep as it is bothering you during the day. Stresses, especially ones you can't control, can dig deep into your unconscious and continue negatively affecting you. Dreams offer a way to deal with them on the deepest level. (If this or other banishing techniques do not work, always seek professional help.)

Goal: To use dream-work techniques to banish deep problems in the unconscious mind.

Procedure: Fixations, worries, and traumas often manifest in dreams as horror situations or monsters of some sort. If you have the same sort of dream several days in a row or encounter the same monster or bad person several dreams in a row, then you can banish them.

1. Before you fall asleep, draw a symbol or an image of what the monster looks like. Take a small knife (a silver one if you have it) and stab the drawing, saying, "I slay this 'demon' by my will!" Keep the paper with the knife through it on your bed-side table.

2. As you fall asleep, visualize yourself as a knight, samurai, glad-iator, or some other sort of warrior with armor and weapons. Hold this self-image as you slip into dream.

3. In the dream, when you are confronted by the nasty, remember your armor, your sword, and your *will*. Do *not* run. Attack!

   It may take a few nights to fully face and attack your "id beast," but once you have, it will no longer have power over you.

4. When you have won, destroy the image and keep the dagger around for future "demon" hunting.

Sigil Banishing Technique

Often the real battle between a "demon"—an anxiety or fear—is centered in the deep or unconscious mind. Since logic and conscious techniques do not work in this realm, we need to use stealth techniques to sink our will deep down and get some deep banishing done. Sigils are a great way to do this.

Goal: To encode a desire, empower it with your will, and sink it deeply into your unconscious to banish (or at least subdue) a persistent negative experience, thought, complex, or obsession.

Procedure:

1. Write out on a piece of paper, in very simple terms, what your will is. It can be anything from letting go of constantly thinking

about of a relationship that haunts you to banishing a mental anxiety. For example: "I will to banish hypercritical thinking."

2. Cross out all the repeated letters. In the example phrase, you would end with: IWLTOBANSHYPERCKG.

3. Let your mind flow and relax. Seeing the letters as forms, play around with them on a piece of paper, fitting them together as you like into a single stick-image, like a rune.

    Once you have this figure, or sigil—you may make many versions until you get it to *feel* right—you are ready to banish it. This sigil is the form of your mental "demon" being banished.

4. Choose a time when you are either utterly exhausted or involved in something so thrilling that you are not really fully in your conscious mind. It might be when you are about to fall asleep on a night when you are up late and so exhausted you can't think properly. Or when you are diving into a pool, riding a roller coaster, having sex—whatever situation where you are really out of it.

5. At that time, pull out this sigil and focus on it. Focus on it like you have never focused on anything before. Forget what it means—just concentrate on it as a symbol until it glows in your mind.

6. At the moment when you are completely fixated on the sigil, destroy it. Forget it completely. Let it go. Never try to remember it again. You have just planted it deep into your unconscious mind.

7. Forget the sigil and the ritual as much as you possibly can.

8. After a week, check in with yourself. What has changed in your life? This is a remarkably effective technique for causing shifts in the deepest layers of the psyche, so the changes may be subtle.

Words of Power Banishing Technique

Since the dawn of prehistory, all peoples have had spiritual and magical traditions concerning words of power. In the Bible and many other holy books, God created the world by uttering a word. Other religious traditions believe that all things and people had a hidden word of power that was their very essence. Whether you are a believer or not, deep in the myth-filled unconscious mind, logic is different and words have power.

Goal: To find a few personal words of power for internal, deep mental banishing and use them to banish inner problems and complexes.

Procedure: To find your word or phrase of power:

• Dig into your religious tradition for words and phrases that banish evil. Even if you consciously don't believe in them, these traditions still are imbedded deep in your unconscious mind. If possible, these words should not be in English (or your native language, but in a "magical" language). If you are Catholic, think of Latin; if you are Jewish, think of ancient Hebrew. Do a little research! Here are some examples:

> Latin: *Nihil est!* ("Be gone to nothing!"). Or from the exorcism ritual: *Tu autem effugare, diabole!* ("You o devil be gone!")
>
> Hebrew: *Tetragrammaton* (refers to the word of God, repels all evil) or *Elohim* (name of God).
>
> Greek: *Apos Pantos Kakadaimonos!* (Be gone all "demons"!)
>
> Hindu: *Phat!* (Pronounced *padt,* like a loud crack; the "thunder bolt," roughly "Be gone!")

• If you don't have a religious tradition, look into your cultural roots (Celtic, Hispanic, German, whatever) for similar words or phrases. Again, this is about working in the unconscious mind where things you may think are illogical have power.

- Make a phrase clearly describing what you're using your will to banish. For example, "I will to banish hypercritical thinking." (This is another form of sigil work. For more information, see the previous Sigil Banishing Technique.) Remove all double letters, ending up with IWLTOBANSHYPERCKG. Now, scramble these letters into a phrase of power, such as, "Botinshc Wepklyrg!" This then is your clear banishing word of power.

  Using your word or phrase of power:

- You can use it when dedicating or blessing a thing, person, or event.

- Say the word aloud when you feel threatened. Feel the vibration of each syllable. It is particularly effective in dreams when you are feeling threatened and overwhelmed. Use it when that particular mental "demon" is obsessing you. Vibrate the word(s) with confidence and power; envision them manifesting in a burst of light and banishing the evil.

Artwork Banishing Technique

Like myths, dreams, and poetry, art opens up a door into the deep mind. That doorway can be used for banishing.

Goal: To focus your conscious and unconscious mind on a particular obsessive problem or issue and use art to banish it.

Procedure: Yes, I know, you are probably saying "I'm not an artist!" Don't worry, no one will see your creation but you.

1. Pick the art form you want to do. For those who can't draw or paint, collage is fun and powerful. Clay, ceramic art, knitting, beading, jewelry making, and any other art or craft can be a positive artistic medium useful in this practice.

2. Sit and quietly meditate. Focus on the problem, thought, or complex you want to banish. Focus not on the ideas or feelings of it, but on the images and symbols it conjures up.

3. Start your art project. Draw, paint, sculpt, cut, paste as you like. Make sure to put into your creation all the mental images that emerged when you meditated on the problem. Many will not be logical, but it doesn't matter.

4. When you feel you have done enough, put your creation away in a plastic bag. Leave it until you again feel this issue is tormenting you. Then, again, quietly meditate on the issue, conjure its imagery, and add those images and symbols to the art project. Continue this process until you no longer are getting strong urges to work on your project. (It may take days or weeks.)

5. Finally, sit and meditate on your finished artwork. You should be undisturbed, relaxed, and in a comfortable place. Stare at it. Do not think about it, but let it flow over and around you. Let the symbols, the images, the colors speak to you. Here is your problem made manifest. It is all locked into the vibrant artwork.

6. With whatever words you want, banish the issue. Tell it to be gone! *Destroy your art!* Stomp it, throw it, burn it, rip it—kill it however you like!

7. When done, bury the leftover bits or drop them into a body of water.

8. Sit, relax, and feel the relief.

Deep Mind Uprooting Banishing

Deep meditation moves us into the gray area between the conscious and unconscious mind. When we reach this level, we have influence on the deep roots of mental issues and intellectual problems.

Goal: To examine the deep areas of the mind through deep meditation in order to uproot and banish specific negative issues, problems, or complexes.

Procedure:

1. Find a place that is comfortable, dimly lit, and where you will not be disturbed for at least an hour. Wear comfortable clothes.

2. Breathe deeply. Relax. Calm down.

3. As your breathing slows and deepens, begin paying attention to your breaths: breathe in for a count of five, hold the breath for a count of five, breath out for a count of five, wait for a count of five before breathing in again. Repeat the cycle at least ten times, more if possible.

4. Imagine you are floating on water. Relax. It is a peaceful pond. Relax. You are surrounded by lotus flowers and lily pads, each of which is a conscious thought or idea. Relax.

5. Sit, breathe with counting, visualize, and meditate on this water pond image for at least ten to twenty minutes.

6. When you are in a truly meditative state, look around at your pond. Find the ugly or diseased-looking lotus flower. Identify it as the fixation or problem or thought complex you want to banish. It doesn't belong in this beautiful pond.

7. When you are ready, let yourself sink down into the pond. (Don't worry, you can breathe underwater.) With every exhaled breath, you sink deeper. The water is clear and green, there are a few fish but nothing harmful. It is beautiful. You are completely relaxed and comfortable. Do not fall asleep!

8. After ten deep breaths, you gently settle on the bottom. You can clearly see all the stalks of the lotuses and lily pads floating above

you on the surface. You can trace their waving stalks down into the mud you are gently sitting on.

9. Meditate there for a time. Relax. Breathe deeply.

10. Find the stalk of the ugly, diseased lotus plant. You can clearly see it; the others are vibrant healthy green, and this one is brownish gray. Trace its roots down from the surface to the mud. Its roots are right next to you.

11. Reach over and dig up the roots. It may take time. Keep breathing. Rip them if you need to! Eventually they will come out of the mud. Let go of them. The broken roots will float to the surface. They are gone. That diseased lily is dead. It fades away.

12. Meditate for a time on how relieved you (and the pond) are.

13. Begin to rise off the bottom. Use ten full breaths to do so. At the tenth breath, you are again on the surface. All the lotuses about you are healthy and clean. The uprooted bad one has floated away. It is gone. Meditate here as long as you like.

14. Return to yourself when you like, refreshed, revitalized, and happy.

Spirit: the Self (Be/Not Be)

We are now about to cross over the line between the psychological and the spiritual. We are entering the integral and self-created nexus of conscious/unconscious minds—a central point that coordinates all and yet is beyond all. Jung calls it the Self; others see it as the soul or the spirit. Some call it the Atman, others the Buddha self, still others call it a guardian angel, totem, or ally. In modern investigations, therapists cite the "voice of conscience" or the guiding feel of intuition. I refer to it as the Self, defined as the personification or symbol of the True Will of the individual.

When you are seeking real balance in your life, the most crucial balance is within you. This balance can be seen as between internal and external, heaven and earth, conscious and unconscious, or whatever yins and yangs you like. We rely on this balancing point to help us in our banishing work. The Self can indeed be an ally and through specific meditative techniques, we can call upon it to help in this work.

Through meditation and a combination of other techniques, this center of your being can be reached. Or, when the raging mental storms and tides are stilled through specific meditations, and this inner mental and spiritual center is reached, the Self can gently show how to banish the inner "demons."

In many ways, meditation is the purest path to mental banishing, because it gently pushes aside the ego, turns down the noise and stress of the inner and outer worlds, and allows the Self's pure signal to get through. By living attuned to this signal, you will naturally receive the information and tools you need to banish and to attract the positive things into your life that you have likely been pushing away without knowing it.

This sort of deep letting go often gets the ship of your life back on course. Your Self will bring the path of what you are doing into alignment with your True Will and help you with what you need to do to be happy, if you only give it a chance. Receiving this guidance requires passively accepting guidance from a source of consciousness and awareness that is beyond the ego—something the ego doesn't like! In a way, this work is akin to banishing the "me" worldview and exploring the real you—what you really need, feel, and want to banish deep inside your soul.

Though they're different, all of the meditations in this chapter have the same focus and rationale. The idea is not to banish this or that issue or problem but to banish the entire "mind" and thus let what the Buddhists call real Mind (capital M) manifest. By removing our always-present intellect and dualistic conceptual framework of I/reality we can reset our mental computer.

Mantra Meditation Banishing

Mantra is the Sanskrit (Hindu) word meaning a sacred set of sounds used to create a holy vibration towards a spiritual goal.

For mental banishing, think of a mantra as a tape loop that keeps the focus of the thinking on something other than itself. Just as doctors will distract patients before sticking them with a needle, a mantra keeps the focus off the thoughts and so allows the true Mind to manifest.

Goal: To transcend the mind with Mind.

Procedure: For this meditation, you can use a phrase that has no real meaning in and of itself, like "a rose is a rose" or "Mary had a little lamb."

Or you can use a traditional Hindu mantra, such as, *Om mani padme hum* ("the jewel in the center of the lotus"), *Om Namah Shivaya* ("praise to Shiva Om"), or even just *Om* (Shiva, the original vibration in the world). Traditionally, different mantras contain divine codes (*bijas*) that call forth different aspects of the divine. *Gam* or *Om Gam Ganipatye Namah*, for example, calls forth the elephant god Ganesh who brings luck and prosperity and removes obstacles.

Or you can pick an affirmation. For example, "All thinking stops, I am clear" or "I am open and free of stress." (In this case, the affirmation will do double duty—it will keep your thinking self engaged and help reprogram you.)

1. Sit in a quiet place, relaxed and free from stress and worries as much as possible. Be comfortable and clear.

2. State out loud, in your own words that you want to banish your thinking self and become open to Mind, to bliss and clarity—say it any way you wish.

3. Begin to repeat the phrase you have chosen out loud for a minute or two until you have it memorized.

4. Move to repeating it silently in your head, like a tape loop—over and over and over. If it helps, visualize a smaller you doing the chanting in your head. Focus 100 percent on the phrase; ignore all other things. If you get distracted, you will find the mantra getting warped or you will forget parts of it. When that happens, begin again. Keep that focus on the mantra!

5. When you finally have to get up and do things, keep the mantra going. Focus your thoughts, feelings, sensations on the mantra. Do this for as long as possible.

You may have to do this entire exercise (steps 1 through 5) on a few separate occasions before you achieve full success. What often happens is that the mantra begins to repeat itself, and you detach from your usual state of consciousness. This detachment is what you are after. Unfortunately, the minute you realize you are detached, that detachment ends, your monkey mind is back in place, and the real world with all its problems crashes in. Detachment takes some practice. Keep it up. Some people have more of a knack for detaching through mantra work than others. Once you have gotten that shift, it will get easier and easier to check out. Enjoy your mental vacations!

Stillness Meditation Banishing

This meditation is very easy to do, yet very hard to maintain, especially in our frenetic world. This makes it more valuable in resetting our thinking.

Goal: To banish agitation, sensory overload, excessive irritation, and restlessness.

Procedure: First, find a comfortable place to lie down—a space away from people and distractions, where you know you will not be disturbed. Make sure the room is clean and quiet. If it's not, get a pair of foam earplugs. Silence is really helpful. Eliminate all possible interruptions, such as phones.

Wear comfortable clothing. Make sure you eat a good, healthy meal with lots of protein before you begin.

1. Lie down. (It is traditional to have your head facing north). Breathe deeply and relax. *Do not fall asleep*.

2. Breathe rhythmically. Breathe in, hold, breathe out, hold, breathe in. Focus on your breathing. Count how many breaths you take. Eventually you will feel your body begin to seriously relax.

3. Let go of all your stress and worry. Let images flow through your mind. Do not hold on to any of them. If you begin to fixate on one line of thought, shift your focus to your breathing until it dissolves.

4. After less than an hour, your body will want to get up. You'll start thinking "OK, I'm done." This is where the real banishing begins.

5. Stay still. Visualize your feet disappearing, just dissolving away. Then your legs. Then your hips and loins, then your hands and arms, then your chest, then your neck.

6. Finally, as you breathe in and out, "see" your face and head dissolve. Your mind dissolves into the void, pure darkness. Only breath is left. Then silence.

   You are utterly still. Utterly absent. Utterly banished.

Note: It may take you four to twelve hours to find perfect stillness. It may also take several tries. The biggest problem is falling asleep. If you do fall asleep, try again another time.

Walking Mind Meditation Banishing

As with the Stillness Mediation Banishing, the trick of this banishing meditation is simple, yet it is not easy to do.

Goal: To banish overload, mental chaos, and multitasking fatigue.

Procedure: It is traditional to do this meditation walking clockwise around a holy spot, shrine, temple, or stupa (Buddhist shrine). In our culture, such spots are a bit hard to find, so the traditional walk is hard to do. The best alternative is to find a tree or area in a park where you can walk this circle and not be disturbed. Dawn is an excellent time.

Before you do the walking meditation, eat properly, take care of any bodily business, make sure you have no distractions (turn the cell phone off), and have free time where no one will bother you. Dress warmly and comfortably; wear your most comfortable shoes.

1. Sit quietly first. Meditate on letting go of everything. Become very aware of your surroundings. Fully and completely concentrate your mind on every detail about you, every leaf, every blade of grass, each cloud and flower. Really focus on your surroundings with your whole mind. Let any other thoughts about your mundane life fade as you utterly focus on the beauty around you.

2. Breathe deeply and steadily. Focus your hearing, sight, and senses of touch, smell, and taste on this place, here and now. *This* is real, nothing else.

3. Once you are in this groove, slowly stand.

4. Begin your walk. Utterly and completely concentrate on that step— how your foot hits the earth, how your weight is distributed, how the grass and dirt shift. Your walk will be slow, intense, focused. Nothing should exist about you except that foot hitting the earth. Even the nature around you will fade away.

Your whole universe will be a step. Then another. Then another. Each step will be an entire lifetime, birth to death. Time will shift. Each step will become an eternity.

You will achieve success when you *are* each step. Mind, body, heart—all gone, banished, forgotten.

5. You may return from this "bliss vacation" any time you wish. When done, sit quietly, again focusing on the beauty surrounding you. Return to being you. Slowly let the craziness of the world reenter your mind.

Refreshed, renewed, face your life.

Floating/Hanging Meditation Banishing

One of the most valuable methods for removing yourself from reality is the use of floating or swinging.

Goal: To use weightlessness (or as close to it as you can get) to free the mind.

Procedure: If you are lucky enough to have access to an isolation tank, use it. If not, there are two options. You can find a pool or pond that has warm water and that you can access at night. It must be absolutely dark—no lights around at all. The weather should be quite warm or even hot. Or you can use a hot tub or bathtub—the larger the better. Ideally it should be one you can freely float in. Fill it with hot water and bath or Epsom salts to aid buoyancy.

1. When you are ready, be completely naked. Relax and meditate on darkness, silence, and space.

2. Enter the water, lie on your back, and float. Breathe in and out deeply. Slow your breathing. Relax. Let the water take all your stress.

3. As you breathe deeply and relax, let all your thoughts float away. See them sink into the water and dissolve.

4. After a time, see yourself dissolve. First your arms and legs, then your body, then your head, and, last, your mind and thoughts. You are floating in space, surrounded by darkness and stars. You are completely absorbed and one with the cosmos. There is no "I," no thought, nothing. Simply exist as timeless and without form.

5. When you are ready to come back, see your body reforming in the reverse order as it dissolved: first your mental identity, then your head, body, arms, and legs. You feel renewed and open and relaxed.

    It is very important that you reenter reality slowly—no loud noises, interruptions, or bright lights. Slowly and gently get out of the water with as little movement and sound as possible. Lie down. Light a candle. Maybe read a bit. Come back into the real world slowly and carefully.

Silent Meditation Banishing

People who wanted to banish the world (and their constantly chattering mind) have been using this simple banishing for thousands of years. If you are religious, it is a time to banish the "small you" and open up to the divine. If you are not religious, it is simply a way to shut off your mind and open up to Mind, or the universe. In any event, it is a nifty break from your life and easy to do.

Goal: To banish the "small you" (ego) and open to the divine; to shut off your mind and open to Mind, to the universe.

Procedure: Find an isolated, quiet place to stay—a cabin in the mountains, a shack on the beach, it doesn't matter. It should be clean, relaxing, somewhere in nature, and have all the amenities you need.

There should be healthy food, restroom facilities, heat, an okay bed, and so on. No beer, booze, or other intoxicants should be present. Tea is fine.

The crucial part is that you should be completely alone and not disturbed for any reason. If you have a cell phone in case of emergencies, make sure it is off. Plan to go there for three days.

1. When you arrive, meditate as you wish on your objective: to shut off the mind, to become silent and clear.

2. Live there as you like, in complete silence. Do not utter *one word* for three days. As the silence grows, extend it to your inner chatter. Let your mind become quiet. Relax, enjoy, be still and silent.

   You can take walks, cook, and even draw. But do not read or write. No words!

3. Meditate in silence at least four times a day: morning, noon, sunset, and night.

4. At the end of three days, write something significant and say it out loud to break your silence. If you are religious, it should be some sort of prayer or meditation. If you are not, it should be some sort of poem or deep statement.

5. Return to the noisy life!

Spiritual Banishing

Spirit is the Other, the manifestation of the holy, the energetic, the divine. It is the mysterious and mystical part of us and our universe. It is within and behind and throughout all we are and do and perceive. I have alluded to a Self; others say soul or atman or Higher Self. Some prefer less spiritual terms such as energy or orgone.

Whatever we call it, however we face it and deal with it, spirit has been the core focus of the art and practice of banishing for centuries. The theory is simple: if spirit infuses our universe, then when something evil or wrong or harmful manifests, it can be eliminated (banished) by removing the spiritual basis or source of that fault, whether it is seen as a force or entity. These forces can be categorized into three types:

Malignant or harmful supernatural beings. Almost every culture in some way believes in "demons," devils, imps, elementals, sprites, and/or dark spirits that cause harm or problems. They may be truly evil, like traditional "demons" that cause sickness or steal kids, or they may be simply alien and enjoy causing mischief and trickery, like dark elves, Japanese oni, and the like. These entities are specific characters personified with a spirit form. Often they are banished by invoking a higher power, by threatening them, or by somehow tricking or diverting them away from causing harm.

Ghosts or the dead. Virtually every culture has ways of banishing those who have died but refuse to leave and for getting rid of the unhappy or evil dead who seek to cause problems or even curse or kill the living. These banishments include freeing trapped souls, blasting the evil shades away, appeasing them, or diverting their attention from the living. There are also a number of ways to banish the pall or energy of death itself.

Negative spiritual or psychic energy. Some places are seen as just bad, emanating evil energy, often due to a past tragic history. Other forms of general negative energy originate from curses—people casting the evil eye or even just directing venomous anger at enemies. Yet another kind of negative energy (or negative chi) can come from negative actions, like anger, hate, "bad karma," or from simply being out of sync with the universe. This negative energy is perceived as bad luck or bad vibes. People who are ill or who have holes in their aura, as well as psychic vampires and the like, are also generators of negative spiritual energy. Banishing this sort of energy can be seen more as deflecting, averting, sweeping away, or cleansing. Often calling for a specific type of banishing called purification, and it takes thousands of forms.

The actual banishing may send the spirit or entity back to where it came from. It may destroy, disperse, or absorb the negative influence or entity. Or it may simply clean (purify) a place or person who has become spiritually tainted in some way.

Spiritual banishing can be also defined as any ritual action that removes or gets rid of something in your life or reality—be it physical, mental, emotional, or spiritual—through spiritual or energetic means. By banishing the underlying energetic basis for a problem, you banish the problem itself. The energetic banishing methods can include everything from prayers to spells and chants to dances and invocations. Any set of actions that is luminous, that has a spiritual or transcendent basis, can be an effective banishing ritual.

Rituals, rites, ceremonies, and other forms of spiritual banishing bypass the conscious mind and the ego; they bypass our view of the physical body and circumvent emotional states. The real and most important activity going on is a clearing of the inner self on all levels. Spiritual banishing can thus work wonders because it supercedes all other sorts of banishing.

Regardless of what form the banishing takes, belief is the key to its success. Simply believing that things have shifted, that negative energy or bad luck has been swept away, changes a person's whole life. Belief, or faith, is a powerful banishing and healing tool. Focused belief, a combination of love and will, can move mountains.

Unlike the other chapters in this book, this chapter begins with some general information and principles. It then explores spiritual banishing techniques connected with each of the five elements. Each elemental section begins with a survey of methods, techniques, and procedures used by shamans, magicians, and priests from many cultures around the world.

The Basics of Spiritual Banishing

When doing any type of spiritual banishing:

- Be clear about the spiritual beliefs and worldview you are operating under.

- Identify the spiritual issue at hand and identify the negative spiritual force(s) involved as clearly as possible.

- Make sure the person or the place involved in the banishing is physically clean.

- Never perform a banishing for a person or a place if there is outright disagreement about banishing.

- Prepare yourself spiritually for the banishing. Pray, fast, purify yourself, meditate beforehand—whatever your beliefs call for.

- The focus, willpower, and love of the banisher is crucial to the success of a banishing.

- At the beginning and the end of a banishing, use prayers, chants, or invocations of your faith that call upon higher powers or your innate divine spiritual power.

- Keep the banishing simple, focused, and one-minded.

- Always gets a reality check from the person for whom you're doing the banishing or from a trusted observer when banishing a place. Such a reality check should reaffirm the need for the banishing and agreement by all on the procedure.

- If one spiritual banishing doesn't seem work, try another. Combine techniques. Be flexible, creative, and intuitive.

- After a banishing, call forth positive spiritual, mental, physical, and emotional energy to heal and help. Replace the negative with positive.

Visualization

Visualizing, or seeing in your mind, the spiritual forces and banishing going on is crucial to the effectiveness of all banishing, as is belief that the banishing will work. All the tools, herbs, symbols, actions, and practices are made effective by clear visualization and belief.

As you do a banishing, you (and anyone who is being purified through banishing by you) need to create and follow your own visualization script. Often this script looks like so:

1. See with the mind's eye the negative energy. Often it is dark, colored gray or brown, or looks like cloud. You can also visualize it as an evil entity, ghost, or monster, depending on your beliefs.

2. As the banishing occurs, see this negative force become agitated and begin to move.

3. As the force of the banishing peaks, see the negative force flee, disintegrate into the air, sink into the earth, burn up in fire,

disperse into water, or be captured in some way. Then it is disposed of.

4. Focus on a positive force, desire, or intent.

Coordinating visualization with prayer, chanting, and ritual actions is the key to all effective banishing. Hint: Practice first!

Natural Materials

Many spiritual traditions say that special herbs, plants, flowers, stones, earth, and other natural materials used in a banishing should be gathered at a special time. Often the new moon day; a power day like an equinox or solstice; or a holy day like All Souls' Day is recommended.

Also, the knife, scissors, or blade used for cutting plants is said to be important. Do not use iron. Silver or gold seems preferred, though many sources mention aluminum as a good, neutral metal to use. Again, these are simply traditional beliefs, but intent is crucial to a banishing and preparations are a key part of focusing intent.

Banishing Activities: The Elements

There are many kinds of banishing but they can be generally viewed through the lens of the five elements. Thus when contemplating a spiritual banishing ritual, first meditate on what element would be the most appropriate to use in this particular situation, what seems most appropriate, or simply which feels right? Does the negativity stem from a physical issue in the home or in the body? Does it feel fiery and powerful or watery and emotional? This is the place where interpreters of the sacred, shaman, priests, diviners, and others bring experience and intuition to bear. In many traditions, it is the omens, the gods, the spirits, or the "ally" which indicate or whisper the appropriate banishing for *this* problem here and now.

So, no matter what spiritual banishing you seek to do, first: sit and think.

Feel the problem, meditate, open up your intuition. If you consult oracles, do so. If the banishing is of a place or thing, think about the forces involved, what element seems right to counteract or eliminate that negativity? A nasty dark energy might call for a light and fire, a sad depressing gloom may call for an air banishing with smoking sage. Deep emotional pain may call for a banishing bath, and banishing the old vibes from a used car might call for the Earth banishing with some rock salt or a sachet of "earthy" herbs.

Before undertaking the procedure, ask yourself three questions, then look through the elemental sections of the rest of this book and see what feels right:

1. What is the nature of the entity/energy to be banished?

2. Do I choose a kind (element) of banishing that is the opposite of that negative force or, which is similar? (both are traditional) one.

3. Looking at the options, which *feel* right?

Each kind of banishing ascribed to an element has certain activities or actions that are sacred to it. When these actions are performed with focus and intent, they can be effective in banishing rituals. The following is a general procedure for using activities for banishing; see the sections on "Actions for Spiritual Banishing" in each section of this chapter for more specific ideas.

Procedure:

1. Find a suitable time and place to perform the action.

2. After focusing on your problem and intent, centering yourself, and so on, offer an appropriate prayer, chant, or sacred words. Visualize

or call forth the banishing power of the specific element you're working with. For example, clouds for Air, flames for Fire, rain or the ocean for Water, trees for Earth, shining light or void for Spirit.

3. Do the activity with full-focus intensity, visualization, and appropriate actions. While doing it, repeat a prayer or chant or affirmation over and over.

4. At the peak of the ritual, banish the negative energy via that elemental force. Depending on the element, the evil may be seen to burn, drift away, disperse, or sink into the ground. See the various sections.

5. Affirm that the negative energy has gone with joy and positive spiritual actions and words! Give thanks to the heavens. Give thanks to the elemental energies that aided you through gesture and deed. Touch the earth and give thanks.

6. Clean, eliminate, bury, burn, or toss away most excess herbs, etc., used in this rite. Be silent. Go.

Tools

Sacred tools are only sacred (and useful for spiritual rites) if they are treated and honored as such.

- Whenever possible, tools should be handmade or found by the banisher. Making the tools follows the same spiritual steps as charging already noted. Intent, focus, and prayers, chants, and sacred words make the item special as it is created.

- Keep your spiritual tools in a sacred place: a special drawer; a box wrapped in a special, natural-fiber cloth; or another special place or container.

- When a sacred tool breaks or wears out, or when its usefulness has ended, return it to nature with prayers or chants and honor. Leave it outdoors, burn it, sink it, or bury it, but never just throw it away.

- Every time you use a sacred tool, honor it, recharge it, visualize its power, and embrace it as divine. In this way the spiritual force within the item is said to grow and gather and become very strong. Many cultures believe in this, and some such tools are handed down for generations.

- Use the tools in combination with other items, actions, rites, prayers, chants, and so on. Be creative and spontaneous. If you have a specific banishing planned and suddenly are inspired to grab and use a tool, do it! Let the spirit move you.

- Keep you tools clean, both physically and spiritually.

Charging

In a spiritual ritual like banishing, the force and power of the banisher and the collected items, words, and actions cause the positive spiritual effect. Therefore, all items should be purified, centered, and charged with potent spiritual power. Charging means imbuing an item or substance with a charge of potent positive spiritual energy before banishing.

Charging can be done a number of ways, depending on your spiritual reality. Some of the most common ways to charge an item are:

- Holding it in your hands and directing spiritual energy into it with a prayer, chant, sacred song, or mantra.

- Placing the item in a sacred spot (such as the altar of a church, on a large crystal, or in an ancient ruin) and leaving it there for a period of time.

- Getting the item from a person or place (such as a Botanika, the hands of a priest, or a sacred field or well) that has already charged them.

- Letting them absorb a charge from a celestial or terrestrial body. Leave the item in the sunlight, moonlight, or starlight for a period of time, or place it on a sacred mountain, in a sacred cave, or in a sacred spring.

- Sleeping with the item under the pillow, in contact with your body.

- Using other forms of energy such as sexual energy, magnets, or "orgone accumulators."

Air

Many forms of smoke and incense have been used throughout the ages, both to banish an area of malignant energies or beings and as offerings to the gods or spirits. It is hard to think of a single church, temple, or sacred shrine that does not have a form of incense burning in it. Many Native Americans, especially those from the Great Plains, use wild sage wrapped into smudge sticks to drive away evil. In the rite of the peach pipe, the pipe is extended to the four quarters of the world, cleansing the participants and ritual area and giving offering to the Great Spirit.

The Mayans used herbs and copal when clearing a temple of negative beings. Tibetans use a special mixture of herbs and resins, as well as pine boughs, to banish "demons" and wandering ghosts and to make offerings to the gods, Buddhas, spirits, and ancestors. The Catholic and various Orthodox churches use their own sacred blends of resins, such as frankincense and myrrh.

Some traditions incorporate air into banishings by using fans. In Shinto, a wand of paper streamers and rice straw is waved above the space or people involved in the banishing. Tibetans use prayer flags and bells, while in other Asian faiths, Taoism for example, a sacred fan with spiritual symbols is waved about to purify an area.

Various forms of breathing, exhaling, rhythmic or, "dragon power" breathing are used in some traditions. Think of pranayama, or breath work, in yoga.

The Kwakiutl or Bella Bella Native Americans of the Northwest use ceremonial whistles to banish unwanted spirits and call desired spirits. Each whistle is keyed to each function; each tone or note summons or banishes certain things. The Hopi and other tribes of the Southwest use a variety of airborne substances to banish and purify. Corn pollen is sacred and is seen as the life essence that keeps the tribes alive. Plains and central Native Americans use eagle down and a number of other feathers and feather products to purify in a variety of ways. The sacred bird that brings blessings and removes uncleanness, problems, or evil, is a prolific myth around the world, and bird fetishes (feathers, down, talons) or imagery appear in many cultures.

Many cultures use windswept places such as mesas, cliffs, and mountaintops as sacred spaces. The wind is recognized and invoked as an instrument of purification. Many cultures throw various powders into the wind to swirl and purify people and places. In India during the Holi festival, colored sandalwood powders are tossed and blown about, mixed with the sacred mantras and shouts. In many different cultures the final purification of a person who has died, the final release of that person from this world, is in the form of ashes scattered into the wind.

The Vanuatu tribe in central Africa has a unique and very effective purification involving air. They climb very tall structures and, after looping a resilient vine about their ankles, leap off. They plummet headfirst until the vine stops their fall only a few feet short of the ground, and they bounce up and down until they settle. Bungee jumping uses bridges instead of poles and modern rubber and plastic ropes instead of vines, but can give the same cleaning experience.

Swings have been used ritually for purification for thousands of years. In Indian mythology Krishna and Radha are often pictured on swings, and all over India festivals and rites dedicated to these two use swings. In Bangkok, Thailand, up until thirty or so years ago, there was a huge swing purification festival dedicated to Shiva. In the West, certain swings, sometimes known as witch cradles, were early sensory deprivation tools. In many shamanic traditions, before initiation or illumination, the shaman-to-be must dangle from poles on a sacred lodge (as in the Sun Wheel ceremony of the Plains Indians) or hang from a tree upside down (as in the Odinic mysteries of the Norse). All of these methods of personal purification and banishing use the imagery of air and wind to open the psyche, to blow away unwanted ideas and conditioning. Thus the mind and soul are left as clean as a windblown cliff.

Australian tribal people use bullroarers to purify an area, call spirits, and communicate with each other. The bullroarer is a magickal piece of wood (usually) tied onto a string. Whirled overhead, it creates a sacred space of wind and sound that truly sounds like the voice of elementals. Many Pagan peoples wave sacred tree branches to purify an area or people. This ancient rite, which also combines fire and water, is today in Scandinavia called a sauna; among Native Americans it is known as a sweat lodge. The tree spirits and the wind that speaks through their swinging boughs affect the initial cleansing. Inuit peoples (often called Eskimos) toss people in a blanket as high as they can to cast off the bad and bring in the good.

Any and all of these methods can be used today with a little imagination.

Incense and Smoke Banishings

Preparations:

- First, choose the specific incense or smoke; see the banishing herb list at the end of this air section for ideas. Make sure you use the purest form of incense or herb, especially if the banishing involves smoking or smudging. Make sure the herbs have not been sprayed with chemicals and were harvested at the right time astrologically or during the right phase of the moon. If these things are of interest to you, more information can be found in the appendix charts.

- For smudging, the herbs should either be wrapped with a cotton thread or dried completely. For smoking, herbs should be ground up and include no stems. For incense, if using pure herbs or resins, also use a self-igniting charcoal.

- If smudging, catch the ashes in a shell, pottery bowl, or other vessel decorated with protective symbols or symbols sacred to your religion.

- For smoking, use a sacred pipe that has been charged. There is a complex and interesting tradition around Native American sacred pipes and ceremonies using them; investigate this tradition if it interests you, but always honor the particulars of that tradition if you plan to borrow from it.

Procedure:

1. Clear and clean yourself and the area to be banished. Center yourself. Meditate, pray, chant, and so on. If you are doing this banishing for a person, he or she should be seated before you. Face either north or east, depending on your spiritual tradition. (North is the direction of the earthing and banishing; east the direction of the dawn and new beginnings.)

2. Light the herb, plant, or incense. Offer it to the heavens with an appropriate prayer, chant, or other sacred words to the divine.

3. Offer some of the substance to the earth in a similar manner.

4. Offer smoke to the four directions in a similar manner. (Some go to the east, then the south, then the west, then the north; some make a cross and go east, west, south, north. It's up to you.)

5. Direct some smoke in, over, and around yourself with an appropriate prayer, chant, or other sacred words. Enjoy and be mindful of the scent. This is to purify your own mind, heart, and body. If you are doing the banishing for someone else, do the same for him or her. Have the person repeat the prayer, chant, or words with you.

6. Declare (and visualize) the place or person free of all negative or evil influences.

7. Bury the ashes in the ground. Thank Mother Earth.

Banishing With Scents, Fumes, and Smells

Procedure 1 (Fumes):

1. Find an unblemished, organic onion. Charge it. (You can also use garlic.)

2. Cut the onion in half with appropriate prayer, chant, or other sacred words.

3. In small bowls or dishes, take the onion halves, cut side up, to the area affected.

4. Walk once counterclockwise around the area, using appropriate prayer, chant, or other sacred words, plus visualization. Tell the negative energy to go.

5. Leave the onions there for several days.

6. When you feel the onions have absorbed or repelled all the negative energy, take them outside and bury them.

Procedure 2 (Scents): Banishing scents can be in the form of oils, powders, waters (such as rose water), actual flowers, or even a potpourri created especially for this banishing. Oils can be extended with some alcohol. Scented waters can easily be created by making a tea with an herb or flowers. See the list of herbs and banishing scents in the appendix.

1. Decide on the appropriate scent or scent item.

2. Charge the scent or scent item.

3. Make sure the area (and/or person) and yourself are clean. Make sure all doors and windows are open. Center yourself.

4. Offer the scent or scent item to the divine with a prayer, chant, or other sacred words.

5. Inhale the scent or place some on yourself with a prayer, chant, or sacred words. If another person is involved, do the same for him or her.

6. Clearly state what you are banishing, why this scent will get rid of this negative thing, and why the thing must go.

7. Beginning at the doorway, walk counterclockwise about the whole place or the person, letting the scent arise, or sprinkling or waving the scent, depending on its form. Repeatedly exhort the negative force to get out.

8. Make a holy or protective banishing symbol on the walls, doors, and floor with the scent. On a person, mark it on the

9. Leave a small dish of the scent or the scent item in the room— at least one dish facing each of the four directions. Some of the scent may be put in a small bottle or charm and worn on you or the other person.

10. Offer a final and impassioned prayer, chant, or sacred words. Loudly order the negative force to go by the power and virtue of this scent.

11. End with a positive prayer or chant and visualization.

12. Leave the scented dishes or charms in place for at least three days. Then collect or sweep up whatever is left and bury it.

Air Activities for Spiritual Banishing

These actions or activities are associated with the banishing power of air, the winds, and the flow of spirit energies.

• Swinging for long periods of time

• Rocking in a hammock, especially a very enclosed one

• Bungee jumping or skydiving

• Climbing or sitting in trees—the higher the better

• Spinning—usually in one place—for extended periods of time

To use these activities for banishing, follow the general procedure described at the beginning of the chapter. Call forth the banishing power of the wind, storms, clouds, and arching sky. Visualize the negative energy blowing away and dispersing in the wind. Finish by raising your hands to the sky and giving thanks.

Air Tools for Spiritual Banishing

Knives and swords: Ancient ceremonial blades are found in every culture around the world. Long ago, banishing a killer wolf and banishing an evil spirit seemed like pretty much the same operation, and the same is basically true today. Swords or daggers used in banishing are traditionally steel or iron but can also be bronze, silver, and sometimes gold. Such weapons are often key tools in many traditions, from Wicca to Tibetan Bon Po shamanism, and each individual has his or her own blade, athame, purbah, or what have you. Most of these traditions use the blade to banish—traditionally threatening, killing, stabbing, or driving off evil spirits. Such knives are also used to banish hungry or lost ghosts by cutting them free of their attachments to this reality. Swords are said to have souls and must be treated with respect. In ancient grimoires, magicians could often banish merely by grabbing the sacred sword's handle and posturing. Swords and sacred knives often have special words of power, runes, or symbols inscribed on their blades or handles.

Feathers: All kinds of feathers are powerful and sacred and are used within a variety of traditions. The best are ones you find. It is always better to find feathers than buy them, but if you buy them, make sure that they are not dyed and haven't come from a bird that was unnaturally treated or killed. *Do not* use illegal feathers, such as eagle feathers, often they came from poachers—bad karma indeed. Different birds and their feathers have different symbolic meanings. Thus, different feathers may apply to different banishing situations. For strength and power, use hawk feathers; for domestic stresses and fights, use rooster feathers; for love issues, try dove feathers; for luck and money issues, duck or goose feathers are said to work.

Fans: All kinds of fans, foldable and nonfoldable, are used in many banishing ceremonies around the world. Most are made of bamboo, wood, and paper. Other kinds—such as those made of sandalwood, silk, feathers and leaves—are inherently powerful and used in rituals such as banishings. If you are making your own sacred fan for banishing, you will either make it from scratch or buy a blank one and add to it. Simply taking a piece of paper, folding it a number of times and stapling or taping one end works. Color your fan the appropriate color for your use and paint or draw an appropriate banishing symbol on it. (See the air symbols list in this chapter.)

Flags or banners: These are, in many ways, very similar to fans as magical tools. The main differences are that flags are almost always made of cloth and just hanging them is often enough to chase away evil forces. Flags or banners may announce the presence of a god or goddess that scares all evil away (like in Voodoo), or they may have images that generate prayers (like Tibetan prayer flags) and thus banish negativity. Or the flags may have specific words or symbols that basically say "get out" to bad spirits. Others, like some Taoist flags, are "activated" by waving them about.

When using banners, you have three options. First, you can buy, charge, and hang banners or flags for ongoing banishing and protection. Second, you can create or alter specific flags for your own ongoing banishing; charge them and hang them up at an appropriate time and place. Third, you can create a specific flag and attach it to a pole for specific banishing rituals. Then either destroy the flag or put it away for later ritual use.

Whistles: Whistles have been used in many different cultures to either call or banish spiritual energies. Again, you can easily buy or make a whistle. Homemade whistles are often crafted from wood and often have other symbols and colors worked into them. Again, the use of the whistle determines the form and that is up to you. Metal whistles, of course, can be made from a variety of materials, and they also have symbolic meanings.

Another important consideration is the note or pitch of the whistle. Some people assert that hypersonic dog whistles work very well when banishing evil spirits. Flutes, pipes, and so on can also be used. Blasting one note or a sacred series of notes (a banishing song) is part of this tradition. When whistles are used, they are often blasted to the four directions and accompanied by prayers and chants to order the evil spirits to go. There is evidence that the shock of the whistle jolts people, thus aiding the banishing.

Wind chimes: All kinds of chimes—ceramic, metal, glass, bamboo, and even silver or gold—can be found or created to banish unwanted forces or entities. Often these wind chimes have banishing or protective symbols crafted on them. Once put up, they let the wind activate them to perpetually generate spiritual action. You can create or buy a set of wind chimes and charge them up for the intended banishing. Inscribe a specific symbol or set of symbols on them to accomplish this goal, then hang them up at an appropriate time and place and let the wind do the rest.

Bullroarer: This is an Australian aboriginal ritual tool. It is simply a flat, oval-shaped piece of wood, often marked with sacred symbols, with a hole at one end. A cord is tied through this hole. You swing the roarer overhead in ever widening circles as you let the cord out. At a certain velocity, it begins to roar, making a wild, haunting sound that can be sped up or slowed down by how fast you swing it around. Clearly, the ritual possibilities are endless. You can make one out of a variety of woods or other materials, then paint or inscribe banishing symbols on it.

Breath: In many different cultures, banishings and exorcisms are accompanied by the banisher blowing on the affected area/place. Often shamans, healers, priests, and so on blow through hollowed bones, bamboo, sticks, and other items. Often these items are marked with sacred signs and symbols. Sometimes these blow tubes are used to blow around other sacred banishing substances, such as pollen, down, or sacred dusts. You could use all of these concepts to create sacred blow tools, but, using creative visualization, you can also just blow away the bad forces.

Key Air Symbols for Spiritual Banishing

Symbol	Meaning
Feather	Truth, justice, and balance
Spiral	Creation, turning or drawing inward, origins, life, healing
Wind (spirals, wavy lines, cloud forms)	Purification, clearing away, movement
Sword/Dagger	Power of the mind, force, intensity, command
Birds	Freedom, spirit, transcendence, purity (Note: Specific species can have specific meanings.)
Butterfly	The soul, movement, evolution, rebirth
Leaves	Renewal, healing, and spirit power (Note: Specific kinds can have specific meanings.)
Flowers	Healing, blessing, growth, renewal (Note: Different kinds have specific meanings.)

Fire

In India, amidst the loud chanting and throbbing music of a festival, dozens of people sway back and forth in ecstatic trance as the flames die down. Suddenly they walk forward across the burning coals. Some dance, and others pick coals up and put them on their tongues. Their flesh is not burned, and there is no pain.

In Japan, near New Year's Day, a group of Buddhist monks in white robes chant the Lotus Sutra and bang gongs repeatedly. Suddenly several of them pick up burning sticks and begin to rub them all over their bodies. Some of them place these brands in their mouths. There is no pain; there are no wounds.

Rites similar to these occur all over the world; fire walking has become popular even in Western countries. It is a form of spiritual banishing.

Fire, the source of light, the origin of civilization, may be the most powerful and potent purifying force. In countries of Celtic and Scandinavian traditions, the need fires, or great sacred bonfires, are kindled on mountaintops at the sacred festivals. Often people leap over the fires at the peak of ritual excitement. This scary and potent leap purifies the spirit and banishes all bad luck. In cultures where cremation is the norm, fire frees the spirit or soul; it removes dross and reduces matter to its essentials. In fact, burning a thing leaves nothing but the salts and carbon associated with earth, a potent mystical element in and of itself.

In alchemy the sacred fire used in the magnum opus was called the *Alkahest*. It was not just seen as the tool for chemical and industrial development that it later became. It was also seen as the spiritual will, the passion and power of the human and divine essence that transmutation made possible. The ancient Hebrews called this primordial universal fire Qadosh, and the Vikings called it Muspelheim.

Fire is what protected people from the Great Beast—the wolf, saber-toothed tiger, bear, or lion—that was always lurking outside the circle of light at night. Volcanoes, those meetings of fire and earth, are always sacred; people climb them, bathe in their fumes, and sacrifice to them.

One common form of purification seen in thousands of places is the symbolic burning of prayers, sins, and desires in the sacred fire. In Japan a paper doll is rubbed over the body to absorb evil and then it is burnt with prayers. In Tibet branches and butter images are burnt as offerings and to banish evil. Many cultures mark the New Year by thoroughly cleaning and eliminating amulets, charms, and other things in a sacred fire.

Candles, fires, lamps, and torches have always been an important part of almost every spiritual ritual. Mystics and others peer into the fire to see the future or to commune with spirits and gods. In the Chinese culture, the noise and flame of firecrackers and rockets drive off evil spirits and banish misfortune. Birthday candles—today seen as extinguishing old age—were once a potent form of banishing evil and wishing for good. Energy and matter can never be destroyed, only transformed from one into the other. Thus the flame is extinguished but really transformed; it is gone from our perception and takes our wish, prayer, or sin with it.

Fire is often considered the essence of all things. As Hereclitus said, "All is fire." Many philosophers agree and, if we consider fire the outward symbol of all energy, so do modern scientists. Kundalini, as shakti or power when activated, is said to bathe the aspirant in the purifying fire of consciousness. Simply visualizing the human aura as light causes the body's temperature to rise and the blood to flow more quickly.

Candles, lamps, and fires are lit in many rituals for an even simpler reason: the sacred light, just by its existence, banishes the dark, the realm of shadows. Nothing does this better than the sun. The sun may be the source of all energy and all purification, and most cultures have seen fire as the "little sun" or "the son of the sun."

Herbs such as sage, bundles of cedar bark, sacred lamps of oil, candles with runes carved into them, and combustible images—all of these and more are traditionally burned to spiritually banish negative energy or purify an area or a person.

The Vajra wand of Tibet symbolizes lightning, which possibly was the origin of all fire millennium ago, the fire from heaven. In many traditions any sudden burst of neurological energy is referred to as lightening. The simple banishing in Tantrika—striking the palm of the left hand, often while shouting out the power mantra "phat"—is called "the lightning bolt" and is very effective.

Fire is motion, action, dance; the leap of the flames finds echoes in many sacred dances, which purify, charge, and banish the mundane.

Often the simple presence of fire is enough to cleanse or banish an area for ritual work; the imagination is aflame with possibilities!

Fire and Flame Banishings

Preparations:

- First, choose what kind of fire or flame you will be using and whether you are banishing an area or person. Suggestions for what kinds of woods, herbs, oils, and other materials to use in lamps, fires, or candles can be found in the charts and correspondences at the end of the book. Whatever kind of fuel you choose, make sure to use the purest form, especially if the banishing involves being close to the fumes. Make sure the woods, oils, herbs, or whatever have not been sprayed or made with chemicals and were harvested appropriately.

- For fires, the woods or herbs should be cut into small, easy to ignite lengths.

- Unless fires are lit in a hearth or fire pit, they must be in a metal or ceramic container. Make sure that this container will not crack. (Glass can shatter or crack and is not an appropriate container for this.) Appropriate symbols are often painted, glazed, or inscribed on the fire container. Use whatever symbols are right for you, such as those from your religion or one of protection.

- A number of tools can be used in banishing with fire; see the "Fire Tools for Spiritual Banishing" section for ideas.

- Sacred fires are a ritual that goes way back into prehistory. Do a little research. You will find facts about the best time to build certain fires and other traditions. For example, in Celtic cultures, ancient "need fires" were burned on Lammas, or August 1, to banish evil and to purify.

- *Always* have a bucket of water nearby any time you use fire for banishing.

   Procedure:

1. Clear and clean yourself and the area to be banished. Center yourself. Meditate, pray, or chant. If you are doing this banishing for a person, he or she should be seated before you. Face south—the direction of fire, strength, power, and command, all the things you marshal in fire banishings.

2. Charge the woods, herbs, or other fuel you've chosen.

3. Light the fire. Offer it to the heavens with an appropriate prayer, chant, or other sacred words to the divine.

4. Offer some ashes or shine the light to the earth in a similar manner.

5. With your back to the fire, let the fire energies fill you. Extend them out by opening your arms to the four directions with a

prayer or chant. (Some go to the east, then the south, then the west, then the north; some make a cross and go east, west, south, north. It's up to you.)

6. Feed the fire, continuing to pray or chant, while invoking the divine *within* and *as* the fire. Focus on how the fire turns matter into energy and transforms.

7. Once the fire is going, wave the heat of the flame in, over, and around yourself with an appropriate prayer or chant to purify your mind, heart, and body.

   If you are banishing with someone else, do the same for him or her. Have the person repeat the prayer or chant with you line by line.

8. Burn whatever you want to be rid of. Toss appropriate symbols, writings, items, herbs, or whatever into the flames. Pray and chant continuously. Do a lot of fire visualization—see the fire renewing, refining, burning away all evil.

9. When ready to finish, leap over the fire, south to north, with a loudly yelled prayer, chant, or power word. If you are banishing negative energy from a person, have him or her do the same.

10. Turn and face the fire and declare (and visualize) the place or person free of all negative or evil influences.

11. Let the fire burn out naturally while you pray, chant, or silently meditate on the transformation. (Do not put the fire out with water unless necessary. But do make sure the fire goes completely out.)

12. Bury the ashes in the ground, thanking Mother Earth.

Banishing With Candles and Oil Lamps

Procedure 1 (Candles): Get the appropriate banishing candle. The color (black or white are the most common), size, and especially material are important. Beeswax is preferable to others, such as palm-oil-based candles. Most paraffin candles are made from synthetic oil and are the least powerful.

Candles can contain powerful spirit-enhancing items like scented oils, precious or semiprecious stones, and herbs. Any symbol, word of power, or image can be carved into a candle, making them very flexible spiritual items.

1. Clean yourself and the area completely. If banishing negative energies from another person, make sure they are clean as well. Make sure the candle is in an appropriate and clean candleholder.

2. With prayers, chants, or other sacred words, charge the candle and inscribe appropriate words or images on it with focused concentration and visualization.

3. Optional: Hold the candle up to the four directions and bless it as a fiery tool for banishing.

4. Order the negative force to go. Spiritually link it with the candle.

5. With appropriate prayers, chants, or other power words, light the candle.

6. Let it burn until completely gone.

7. As it goes out, send the negative force away with appropriate prayers, chants, or other power words.

8. If any nub is left, burn or bury it. Honor the Earth.

Note: Candles can also be used to ward off or protect you from negativity, keeping bad things away on a continual basis. This calls for longer-lasting candles with banishing symbols on them. Typical warding candles are red or brown. See the next section on oil lamps.

Procedure 2 (Oil Lamps): Oil lamps add three crucial things to the banishing effectiveness ascribed to candles or fires. First, they are permanent and can be made from symbolically important substances, such as ceramics, metal, or fireproof glass. Second, banishing symbols, images, or words of power can be permanently part of the lamps or inscribed on them. Third, the oil itself can add scent and substance to the banishing involved. See the appendix for suggestions for herbs, oils, and scents.

1. Charge the oil and the lamp.

2. Make sure you and the area are clean. If banishing negative energy from another person, make sure he or she is clean as well. Make sure all doors and windows are open.

3. Center yourself.

4. Offer the lamp to the divine with a prayer, chant, or other power words. Light it.

5. Command the light to represent the divine to drive out the negative force.

6. Meditate on the light as the focal point of divinity. The light pervades all things.

7. When the room is full of light, heat, and the scent of the oil, wave the heat of the flame in, over, and around yourself using your hand with an appropriate prayer or chant to purify your mind, heart, and body. If you are banishing something from

someone else, have him or her do the same. Have the person repeat the prayer or chant with you line by line.

8. Optional: Use the flame of the lamp to burn papers with appropriate symbols, writings, or herbs that signify whatever you want to be rid of. Pray or chant continuously. Do a lot of fire visualization—see the fire renewing, refining, burning away all evil.

9. Clearly state what you are banishing, why this lamp and flame will get rid of this negative thing, and why it must go.

10. Beginning at the doorway, walk counterclockwise about the whole area or around the other person, letting the lamplight fill every corner of every room. Repeatedly exhort the negative force to get out by the power of the divine light you wield.

11. At the end, offer a final and impassioned prayer or chant and loudly order the negative force to go by the power and virtue of the light.

12. End with a positive prayer, chant, or visualization.

13. Return to the center of the room. Let all the oil burn away or light the lamp every day for a period of time until all the oil is gone.

Note: This same process can be done with a big, long-burning holy candle as well. Keep the candle or lamp charged as the sacred object it is.

Fire Activities for Spiritual Banishing

These activities are associated with the banishing power of fire, divine will, light, energy and the spark of spirit energies.

- Intense activity of any kind: running, weightlifting, playing a sport, and so on—the key is the intensity

- Martial arts katas or sequences—anything that gets the chi moving and erupting

- Fencing, knife throwing, whittling

- Leaping, jumping, lunging

- Suntanning

- Energetic dancing

- Fire walking

- Sadomasochistic sexual activity

- Driving, riding, or piloting anything with an engine

To use these activities for banishing, following the general procedure described at the beginning of the chapter. Call forth the banishing power of flame, fire, the sun, bursting energy, sparks, and bright light. Visualize the negative energy burning away and being consumed in a blaze of light. Finish by dancing and giving thanks.

Fire Tools for Spiritual Banishing

Wands, staffs, and torches: Every magician, shaman, sorcerer, and so on has his or her wand or staff of power, as do kings and rulers. The wand is the symbol of authority and command. Phallic it may be, but every culture that conducts spiritual banishing used some sort of wand or staff, often inscribed with words, symbols, or images of power and authority. It is thought that wands symbolize the backbone or root of the nervous system (the tet symbol of ancient Egypt) or a serpent, the ancient symbol of man's innate power (the kundalini serpent that rises up through the body). The wand or staff is used to command that evil forces leave. It is also often pointed at specific parts of the body or at specific places in order to heal or banish negative forces from them.

Sometimes wands are metal (various kinds), wood, or ceramic, and they often are inscribed and tipped with gems, crystals, and other symbolic items. Keep in mind, a good staff, even from ancient times, was a good helping hand when hiking, a useful tool and a club used in warfare, and for defense from others. A little research will show you more than you ever wanted to know about wands and staffs.

Hearths: The hearth is the most primal fire symbol of all and likely the earliest. Originally the tribal source of light, heat, and protection from beasts, and a place for cooking and serving food, the hearth has immense and complex symbology and mythology wrapped around it. There are hearth gods (Agni) and goddesses (Hertha, Hestia), and often the hearth was the place where home rituals and spirituality manifested through devotion to the divine as flame and through flame. Offerings were and are still often offered in the hearth flame. Symbols or amulets of protection are often left on or near the hearth. The mantel once was an altar and is still in many ways the center of the home. Hearths (and outside patio hearths too) should always be kept clean. To banish negative energy from a home, light and use a special fire in the hearth. Healings and banishings of energies from people can also be done on a hearth using special woods and herbs.

Lamps, candlesticks, and thuribles: Lamps and candlesticks were and are important spiritual tools in many traditions. Key images and symbols can be inscribed on them or be part of their fashioning. The objects themselves may also be symbols. I've seen a lamp in the shape of a phoenix (a symbol of life, power, and renewal) and a human skull used as a candleholder. Both were used in banishing rituals, though in very different traditions.

Jack-o'-lanterns: Lamps made of turnips or pumpkins go back to ancient times. On All Hallows Eve in ancient Celtic Europe and England, when the dead came back to be honored, the flame led them home. But afterwards, the flames again were lit to send them off. Often bonfires ended this visit, and with good reason—no one wanted the dead hanging around. Similar customs can be found in a number of divergent cultures.

Firecrackers and fireworks: For centuries fireworks and firecrackers were used in China as a magical or spiritual banishing tools. The flash, noise, and jolt they gave were perfect for scaring evil spirits away. They are still used this way—simply go to any lunar new year celebration and you will see the Shi Shi (fire lions) dancing to chase out evil and long strings of exploding firecrackers filling the air. People use firecrackers and flash powder in banishing rituals all the time. Any fine powder (including flour) tossed into the air over a flame will create a flash burst. *But be careful!* Fire is fire and inherently dangerous. Firecrackers can hurt flesh and start fires. If they are illegal where you are, don't use them. Be safe and be smart.

Guns: While I hesitate to mention guns, they simply can't be left out. Guns have such a powerful hold on the collective psyche that they have become powerful tools, even if never fired. A recent study showed that just handling guns heightens hormones and aggressiveness in men. Today, several god forms are connected with guns (the African god Ogun, for example) and even their image is a potent symbol. Guns with blanks in them have been effectively used to banish nasty entities. If hanging up a gun or using one in a ritual is your thing, be safe. Follow all the basic gun-handling rules and never point one (even one loaded with blanks) at someone.

Ashes: Ashes from "power" fires or sacred dhunis (Tantric fire pits) have been used to heal and bless and to banish ills and bad luck for centuries. Placing sacred ash on your forehead on Ash Wednesday banishes sin and is a mark of grace. Placing some over your doorway banishes evil spirits. Holy men and women, in many varied faith, use ashes on their body as a sign of divinity, atonement, or purification. A classic Buddhist meditation has one sit in the cremation ground (where corpses have been burned) and wear ashes in order to let go of ego attachments. Whatever fire ritual you perform, especially if banishing, the ashes of your fire are considered a powerful tool by many. At the very least, they should be buried or given back to nature.

Fire-juggling devices: I have seen modern banishing rites that use fire-juggling items. Made of metal, these can be chains with balls soaked in flammable liquids, wheels—well, almost anything. People light them (usually at night) and swing them about, roll them along a flaming path, and so on. It is a powerful spectacle and, I have been told, a very old banishing practice. In ancient times, wheels of burning hay were rolled down hills to banish negative energy from outdoor areas, and in Japan they run down mountains with huge flaming wands to chase evil away. Certainly these ideas are—*with tremendous caution and preparation*—adaptable.

Key Fire Symbols for Spiritual Banishing

Symbol	Meaning
Wand	Power, authority, virility, strength, passion, defense
Triangle (pointing up)	Light, flame, divinity, balance, enlightenment
Torch or flame	Purification, illumination, guidance, protection, power
Red or Gold Serpent	Wisdom, protection, force, empowerment, kundalini
Phoenix	Rebirth, renewal, long life, chi, female royal energy
Dragon or salamander	Spirit of fire, royalty, power, energy, heaven

Sun (Lightning)	Power, enlightenment, healing, authority, light
Eye	Divinity, insight, focus, rulership, the Self, defense

Water

Almost all religious and spiritual traditions use water in one way or another as a purifying medium.

As Tibetan monks prepare for a puja (ritual of devotion) to Tara or Mahakala, they pour water from a silver vessel, suck it into their mouths, and, after swishing it around, spit it out, often with a mantra.

In Japan every Shinto shrine has a water trough with sacred emblems on and over it. Before entering the shrine, one must take a dipper of the water and wash the fingers of both hands and also clean out the mouth before proceeding.

As deep meditation and chanting continue in an ashram in India, the guru walks about the people and, using a beautiful peacock-feather fan wand, performs "shaktipat" and sprinkles/purifies the people, saying "Om Namah Shivaya!"

A Greek Orthodox priest, chanting sacred prayers takes an aspergillum from the altar and sprinkles holy water over the sacred area before the ritual proper commences. A simple sprinkling of water or a light washing of hands and mouth are practical and brief substitutions for the most common method of banishing with liquid: ritual submersion in water.

The Zen monk sits under the icy waterfall for two days, washing away attachment.

A thousand miles away, hundreds of people are chanting to Shiva and immersing themselves in the Ganges River, whose blessing, they believe can wash away sin and attachment.

A Baptist preacher submerges the girl in a river, baptizing her, cleansing her of sin, and bringing her into the faith.

A Cherokee Indian, three days into his fast, stands in a stream washing away the veil between himself and his vision.

In New Zealand the Maori tribesmen have just finished the three days of a funeral vigil. Several of them go to the deceased man's home and sprinkle every corner with water while chanting. In this way the contamination of death is dispelled.

The Orthodox Jew sprinkles sacred herbs into a bath of hot water while chanting a Hebrew prayer. He will bathe before doing his ritual. A Tantrika magician half a world away is doing almost the same thing, except the herb he is using is Tulsi and the chant is "Aim."

Whether it is done in a sacred African river or in a candlelit bathtub, the process of banishing by bathing is similar. The medium is not just water, but sacred water. It is water that has either long been accepted as sacred (like the Ganges) or has been made sacred with herbs, oils, salts, minerals, a sacred object, mantras, prayers, and so on. Other practices such as gestures (mudra) may also be used. Emerging from the bath, the bather is renewed, clean, and free of negative energy.

Why is this bathing ritual so prevalent? Possibly it is because we are created in the water of the womb. Genetic memory, via the ever-handy group unconscious mind, tells us that we came from the primal ocean. Plus, our bodies are, over 75 percent water, and the constant need to replenish that personal supply is a key factor in human life. In almost all creation and destruction myths, water plays an important part.

Water from the sky has always been seen as sacred, not to mention important for raising the crops that kept the people alive. Rain has also been seen as the sacred sexual fluid that comes from the mating Sky Father and Earth Mother (or vice versa, in the case of Egyptian mythology), and rainstorms always heralded a change in weather, attitude, tension, and emotions.

Aspersing (Sprinkled Water) Banishing

Procedure: If you are adding herbs, oils, or other things to your water, do so well before the banishing. Also charge the water mixture beforehand.

1. Clear and clean yourself and the area to be banished. Center yourself. Meditate, pray, and/or chant. If you are doing this banishing for a person, he or she should be seated before you. Face west, the direction of water, release, purification, letting go, and so on—all the powers you are focusing on this banishing.

2. If you are just using water, hold the container and charge it now.

3. Open the water container. Offer some water to the sky and sprinkle a bit at your feet, all with suitable prayers, chants, or other power words.

4. Optional: Hold the water up to each of the four directions and sprinkle a bit to the north, south, east, and west with suitable prayers, chants, or power words.

5. Meditate on the cleansing properties of water. Bless yourself with the water by touching a drop of it to your head, heart, and loins. If you are banishing someone else, do the same for that person. Have the person repeat the prayer or chant with you line by line.

6. Going counterclockwise, circle the person or area and flick water all over while praying or chanting. Strongly visualize the negative forces fleeing the power of the holy water. Do this around the whole area and/or person three times.

7. When you are finished, face west and loudly declare (and visualize) that the place or person is free of all negative or evil influences.

8. Place the container of water on the floor (or have the person hold it) and point to it. Declare, with a prayer or chant, that any leftover negative forces are now fixed in and absorbed by the water. Visualize this. Cover the water.

9. Carefully pour out the water at the base of a tree, thanking Mother Earth. Make sure you don't mess with it. Then, in running water, wash out the container and let it dry outside.

Note: A number of tools can be used in banishing with water, including special containers.

Wash Banishing

Banishing with a wash is essentially the same banishing by aspersing, except that instead of sprinkling water about, you systematically wash the whole area, home, occasion, or person.

Magickal or purifying washes are often sold in botanikas or New Age/occult stores. They are a part of many Afro-Hispanic religious traditions such as Santeria, Voodoo, and Candoble. You will find small bottles of liquid with names like "unhex wash" or "lucky wash." You may want to experiment with these.

Two other famous washes for banishing negative forces are Florida water (a citrus-scented cologne) and rose water; both can be bought as is. Many shops also carry various herb-infused waters; lavender and mint are popular. These too can be used for banishing washes.

To make your own wash, decide what you want to banish, then choose the herb, mineral, or other substance you wish to add to the water. At an appropriate time and place, such as a new moon night, add these things to pure water in a clean container that has a cover.

Combine the water and substance with focus, will, intent, and suitable prayers, chants, or power words.

Depending on what you are banishing, you may want to charge this water in variety of ways. Some leave it out in the sun for several days; some leave it open to the full or new moon for a couple of nights. Some magnetize the water by placing a magnet, gem, or crystal in the water or under the container for a period of time. Be thoughtful, creative, focused, and look at the appendix for ideas.

When ready, follow the aspersing procedures, but instead of sprinkling the water, wash the floors, walls, and (if possible) ceiling with the holy water. You need only do so once. Make sure to use new, clean, white cloth. If you are washing a person, use a clean washcloth.

At the end, pour the water out at the base of a tree and throw away all the cloths used.

Immersion Banishing

You can do an immersion banishing for yourself or for another. It consists of a quick dunk in sacred water and then a lively exit from the water.

Baptism is a form of immersion banishing; the postulant is cleaned of sin and often takes a new name as well as entering a communion of faith. Other forms of immersion banishing rituals have been used for centuries to give a person a rebirth—a potent symbolic action considering the waters of the womb and so on. Immersion banishing may be appropriate for major life shifts as a way to banish the old and be reborn into the new, whatever that new stage may be.

Procedure 1 (Outdoors): Immersion can be in a stream, river, pond, or the ocean, if you want to use natural water. Some traditional places include where two rivers or streams meet, where a spring enters a body of water, where freshwater meets the ocean, and anywhere that the plant life is flush and healthy. The place should *feel* right. This method can be chilly and often makes for a shorter banishing ritual; often people jump in and out and are done.

- Make sure beforehand that the area is clear of any garbage, brambles, and so on. Also make sure that entry and exit from the water will be easy and safe. Make sure the water is clean.

- The person who is banishing him- or herself of negative forces should either be naked or wear very loose-fitting cotton clothing. White or blue clothing is traditional. A towel and a dry set of clothes should be nearby. All should be new and clean.

- Prayers or chants, as well as meditation should precede the immersion. They should be focused and intense, building up to the actual immersion experience.

- At the emotional peak of the experience the person should quickly enter the water, fully submerge, and then arise. Traditionally, the person shouts or yells some sort of power word, expelling with word and, with intense visualization, the negative entity or energy being cast out and swept away by the water.

- The person emerges "reborn" and free from evil. This cleansing and rebirth should be echoed in the prayers and chants that are given now. The person dries off, gets dressed, and, after all has been said and done, in silence leaves. Some sort of prayer/chant should be offered at that time.

- The immersion clothes (if worn) are traditionally discarded or given away later.

  Optional: Sometimes people going through this sort of immersion banishing are anointed with sacred oil after emerging from the water.

Often a sacred symbol is drawn on their forehead. The type of oil used is, of course, symbolic and can represent everything from a healing to a new name and identity.

Procedure 2 (Tub): An immersion banishing can also be done in a tub of specially prepared holy water. In this case, the process can be more private and last longer. Tub water can contain powerful spirit-enhancing items like scented oils, precious or semiprecious stones, or herbs.

The process is similar to outdoor immersion banishing, but with a few differences.

First, decide what you will add to the bathtub. It may be as simple as a handful of salt or as complex as a combination of herbs. If you want to avoid a mess, tie up the herbs in a piece of muslin, like a giant tea bag. Again, look at the appendix for appropriate herb ideas. The room should either be dark or dimly lit; candlelight is perfect.

1. Clean the tub and yourself beforehand. Take a shower, and if you use soap, use pure soap with no added chemicals or perfumes.

2. Fill the tub with very hot water—the hotter the better, as long as it isn't painful.

3. With prayers, chants, or other sacred words, charge the water by adding the herbs, salts, or oils to it. Hold your hands over the water, visualizing the charge entering and filling the water. You may also want to light a banishing candle near the tub. (See this chapter's section on fire.)

4. As you (or another) enters the healing water, naked, you should be praying or chanting.

5. Immerse your body in the water. The entire time you are in the bath, you should be visualizing, praying or chanting, and focusing healing or banishing energies over your body.

Breath deeply and rhythmically; relax your entire body. Stay in the water for at least ten minutes—more if possible.

6. When done, finish your prayer, chant, and visualization.

7. As you emerge, open the drain and clearly state with conviction that the evil force is gone, that the water has washed it away and you are free of it. Be clear and emphatic. As the water drains away, the evil is truly gone. See it.

8. Dry yourself off with a clean white towel. Do not wash again for a day.

9. Close with a final blessing, prayer, or chant of gratitude. Relax, meditate, and take some alone time before moving on. You may choose to combine an immersion banishing with massage, chakra work, or whatever other healing methods you wish.

Note: All kinds of bath items, from bottles of special oils and salts to special cords that bind bath herbs, can be considered sacred tools and treated accordingly.

Sweat Lodge Banishing

Sweat lodges and sweating have been mentioned in terms of banishing health issues, but many cultures, from Native Americans to the ancient Norse and Mayans, saw sweat lodges as a sacred ritual as well.

In many traditions there are clear procedures to doing a ritual sweat. They often include meditations and prayers, fasting or dietary rules, and guidelines for when and how everything should happen. Do some research, and, if possible, have someone who has held them lead it.

Creating a sweat lodge is also in and of itself a ritual. The lodge is often created with saplings, branches, and blankets. A fire is usually built near the entrance. Hot stones are brought into the lodge, and water is drizzled on them to create steam. Sacred chants, stories, and visualizations are often part of the ceremony. People often emerge, jump in cold water, and enter again. Visions and other sacred phenomena are not uncommon.

This is a complex proposal, yet anyone can use the idea to banish. All that is needed is a steam room or sauna and a little privacy. You can even use a public sauna or steam room to banish. The following basic procedures can be adapted and done internally if others are around.

Procedures: Bring with you a clean, new cloth or a small branch of cedar, pine, or a fresh healing herb that doesn't irritate your skin. (Test the branch ahead of time.) It may just be a palm-sided frond if you are using a public sauna or steam room. This cloth, branch, or frond should be charged beforehand.

It is best if you are naked, but you can also wear very loose clothing. White or green is preferable.

1. Do some sort of vigorous exercise with a clear focus on what you will be banishing. Even a brisk walking meditation is fine.

2. Take a shower, but do not use any soaps with chemicals or perfumes.

3. When you enter the steam room or sauna, begin your prayer or chant, either out loud or silently. Turn in one complete counter-clockwise circle and spiritually bless the area with your plant frond as you pray or chant. State (aloud or not) what you are banishing.

4. Breathe deeply. Relax your entire body from top to bottom. Visualizing your pores opening. As you sweat, visualize the nasty energy flowing out of you. Breathe. Flow. Stretch. Repeat.

5. Once the sweat is really flowing, use the branch, frond, or cloth to gently scrape the sweat off your skin, always downward. Begin with your head, work down to your feet. It can be a serious get-the-skin-going scraping or just a gentle symbolic brushing. Make sure it doesn't irritate your skin. You are brushing away the negative energy more than the sweat. Do this at least three times.

6. After ten minutes or when you feel ready, leave the room and take a brief cold shower. Keep your constant prayer or chant going, especially and intensely during the shower.

7. Repeat this process two more times if you can: sweat, brush, shower.

8. With the last shower, end the rite verbally and visually with a final declaration of banishing success. Visualize all the evil flowing down the drain.

9. Dry off; dress in clean, new clothes. Bury the frond or cloth at the base of a tree. Give a final prayer or chant of thanks and thank the Mother Earth.

Water Activities for Spiritual Banishing

These actions or activities are associated with the banishing power of water, as well as with insight, deep wisdom, deep healing, creativity, psychic power, and the flowing of spirit energies.

• Swimming and diving

• Wading in streams and the ocean

• Scuba diving or snorkeling

• Sailing, canoeing, kayaking

• Surfing, waterskiing, floating

• Fishing

- Sitting and/or meditating under a waterfall

- Soaking in hot spring pools (very healing and very spiritual traditionally)

To use these activities for banishing, following the general procedure described at the beginning of the chapter. Call forth the banishing power of water, waves, flow, healing, deep-mind and creative energies. Visualize the negative energy washing away and dispersing in the calm blue or green of the flowing waters. Finish by floating in peace and touching your face with water while giving thanks. When done, pour a little water on the earth to end the rite.

Water Tools for Spiritual Banishing

Shells: Shells have been consistently found in prehistoric burials and ritual centers around the world and, coming as they do from the "great water," are the most obvious water-power tool. Many different goddesses, gods, spirits, and even saints have the shell as their symbol, Aphrodite being the most obvious. A conch shell is a potent feminine-deity symbol and is often made into a trumpet for banishing use. Shells are often used as ritual containers for liquids, solids, and fire and for incense or burning herbs.

Cups, chalices, cauldrons: All of these are really one primal symbol; all represent water and, more importantly, the feminine principle. The chalice or cup has for thousands of years represented the Great Mother, the womb, the source of life, and the yoni. Thousands of myths, from the Holy Grail to the Celtic regeneration-rebirth myth of Cerridwen's cauldron, all attest to the lingering power of this potent tool. As a tool, the cup emanates love, compassion, acceptance, rebirth, revivification, fertility, prosperity, cycles, and purification.

Mirror: The magic mirror has been a crucial tool of shamans, magicians, and priests throughout history. All ancient cultures venerated the seemingly mystical power of mirrors to "show" the truth. The symbol of Venus (♀) is actually a hand mirror and such widely worshipped goddesses as Hathor (Egypt) and Oshun (Africa, Caribbean, South America, Central America) have the mirror as their symbol. There are endless myths and legends about the power of mirrors. Vampires (and originally all evil spirits) can't see their reflections and can be revealed and banished with mirrors. Mirrors are the gateway to the spirit world; we cover mirrors when someone dies so they will not return and haunt us. Walking a charged mirror through a house chases out evil spirits, and gazing into one reveals the truth about the forces in and around you. Magic mirrors are used for scrying, as are shallow dark bowls with various liquids in them. (Scrying is a means of activating the psychic sight to see the future or other place.)

Heart: Hearts made of stone, clay, glass, and so on are symbols of love and of the watery powers. Displayed, offered, shown, or even hung up, if charged with intense love—the most powerful, crucial banishing force there is—they are powerful banishing tools. It is interesting to note that the hearts we have today don't look like real hearts; it is likely that they are again yoni or vagina symbols denoting fertility, sexual love, and prosperity.

Key Water Symbols for Spiritual Banishing

Symbol	Meaning
Spiral (double or single)	Eternal return, origin, birth, primal patterns
Waves (parallel, wavy lines)	Ocean, ebb and flow, blessing, purification, movement
Shell	Trumpet for banishing, feminine deity

Heart	Sexual love, fertility, prosperity
Cup, cauldron	Holy Grail, the womb, intuition, emotion
Mirror	Gateway to the spirit world, banishes all evil
Well, spring	Inspiration, wisdom, deep knowledge, a sixth sense, blessing
Water lily, lotus	Attainment, awakening, blessing, consciousness, love

Earth

Since the dawn of time, people have looked for purification, healing, or blessing from certain places imbued with earth power. Mount Kailash in India, the Batu Caves of Kuala Lampur, Mount Arat in the Middle East, the Grand Canyon in Arizona, and Mount Fuji in Japan—all of these and many other sacred power spots are even today inundated with people looking to spiritually banish or purify aspects of their lives.

Yet the desire for purification need not lead one to the actual place. In an annual ceremony near Tokyo, participants walk down an aisle of sand, thus they symbolically make a pilgrimage to dozens of sacred temples without going very far. Simply having a three-dimensional or mental version of Shri Yantra, a representation of Mount Meru, invokes the purifying force of this sacred mountain. In certain forms of Taoist meditation, the seated self is visualized as the mountain, and, when the identification is intense enough, it banishes unwanted thoughts and creates stillness. (For a key to this yoga posture, read the I Ching hexagram "Mountain over Mountain.")

Mountains can rarely be moved, but stones can, and people have been moving and using them ritually since man began using rituals.

Circles like Stonehenge; the Sacred Wheel in America; the sacred stones in Machu Picchu, Peru; or the stones in Palenque, Mexico, are a few examples. Smaller sacred henges, lings, menhirs, and altars are still being made by shamans, magicians, and priests all over the world today.

Then there are the more personal uses of stones. In Tibet or Nepal, if you climb the sacred hills and mountains, you will find piles of stones with prayer flags fluttering from them. Traditionally, you places a stone on the pile as you pass. Thus you symbolically leave behind a part of yourself, maybe something you don't need to carry, and also leave an offering to the spirits.

The stuff of Mother Earth is sacred to most peoples; it is the flesh and bones of the Great Spirit. Many forms of earth power—including chalk, sand, pollen, rice, and flour—are used for cleansing and creating spiritual spaces. In Haiti veves, or sacred diagrams, are traced in the dirt floor of the temple to purify the area and prepare it for the visit of the loa, or presiding spirit. Hopi people use blessed colored sand to demarcate a sacred area and purify it; often people who are sick or in need of cleansing are placed on this sand painting. The "mud people" of Papua New Guinea plaster colored earth on their faces and in their hair to banish negative energy before rituals. In Tibet huge and complex mandalas are created with colored sand as part of a long and intense ritual to purify and bless all the people in the area. Then plants and minerals are rolled and charged as sacred pills, to banish evil, remove negative karma, and even heal physical complaints. The Hopi and Navaho use cornmeal in similar ways; blue, white, yellow, and red forms are all natural and all used.

In the Middle East and parts of India, a person who is suffering under great grief or under the weight of a great sin often touches the earth, sometimes with his or her head, and may cast dirt over his or her head and body. In India and ancient European cultures, people often cover themselves with sackcloth and ashes, or just ashes. Shaivite ascetics and others in India symbolically remove unwanted ideas and ego attachments by rubbing the ashes of cremated people all over their bodies.

By scattering sacred earth over oneself or a given area problems and guilt are "earthed" and thus removed.

Symbols from within the earth have been used throughout time to banish and manipulate energies. Special stones, especially precious and semiprecious stones, have been found in Neolithic pit burials. Crystals and stones are some of man's earliest sacred objects, used in many cultures to ceremonially purify people and areas.

Double-terminated crystals have been found in burial sites and in sacred places from Scandinavia to Peru. The "wish-fulfilling gem" of ancient Indian Tantrik mythology can not only banish all evil, but also grant all wishes. Australian aboriginal peoples have many inscribed stones that contain so much power that for the uninitiated to look upon them is death. Simply bringing these stones into a given area makes the area sacred. In China certain "singing stones" are powerful tools that produce banishing sounds and energy when struck; sometimes sheets of inscribed jade are used in this way.

Plants and trees are powerful earth-based tools and symbols. In Shinto shrines, branches of bamboo are attached to the Torii, or gates, to purify the shrine and people who enter it. Kwakiutl Indians in British Columbia always tie rings of fresh cedar bark around their arms and necks before their winter ceremony.

The Yule tree, a traditional earth blessing stolen by the Christians from Pagan Norse religion, is a prime example of tree worship and bringing the earth spirit into the dwelling to bless, purify, and empower it. Then the Yule log is burned a symbol of removing the clutter of the old year and cleansing the tribe for a new start at the New Year.

Of course, if you spill some salt, don't forget to toss some over your shoulder! This simple earth-oriented banishing has roots in far antiquity.

Clearly the possibilities for earth-based spiritual banishing are limited only by the imagination and the materials produced and offered by Nature.

Banishing with Earth, Mud, Sand, Leaves, Pebbles, Clay, or Rock Salt

The most obvious ancient banishing ritual of earth is to simply lie in it or put it on you. Today we have mud baths and clay masks at spas, but the spiritual ritual is still the same: earth absorbs and banishes evil forces. Clearly, this banishing is for people removing negative forces from themselves.

Preparations:

- First, choose what kind of earth substance you will be using: dry earth, mud, sand, leaves, small stones, clay, or salt. Your comfort, the type of negative force being banished, and what substances you have nearby may determine your choice.

- Next, decide exactly where to do this ritual. Choose a special, powerful, and private natural setting. A backyard is fine, or woods, or the seashore may be called for. Scout out the place of banishing first before you do it. Even a bathroom may be used for mud.

- Focus on why you are doing this banishing. Is it for physical or other issues?

- If you plan to add other items to the obvious ones, like crystals, special stones, or magnets, charge them beforehand.

- Bring a wool blanket of a dark color for you to lie on if you are doing this in a wooded setting. Set up the lying-down place ahead of time.

- If you using leaves, they should be freshly picked or cut without using steel. Traditionally, when you remove leaves from a plant, you should ask it for blessings and help, and thank it for its contribution with water, a coin, or other offering.

- If you are covering yourself with earth, sand, or clay dig it up ahead of time, removing noxious items. If using mud, add water to the earth ahead of time as well.

Procedure:

1. Clear and clean yourself. Center yourself. Meditate, pray, or chant. If you are doing this ritual for another person, have them do the same.

2. Face north, and when the banishing begins, make sure you are lying down with your head to the north. (Or have the other person lie this way.) North is the direction of earthing, release, solidity, stability, rootedness, and grounding—all the powers you are focusing on in this banishing.

3. Place both hands on the lying-down spot. Begin your prayer or chant. Thank the earth for this blessing.

4. Hold a bit of your chosen earth material (the earth, mud, sand, leaves, clay, stones, or rock salt) up to each direction and sprinkle a bit to each of the four directions with suitable prayers and chants.

5. Meditate on the absorbing and rooting properties of earth. Bless yourself with the earth by touching your hands and top of your forehead to the pile of material. If you are banishing someone else, have him or her do the same. Have the person repeat the prayer or chant with you line by line.

6. Going counterclockwise, circle the lying-down spot three times while praying or chanting. Strongly visualize the negative forces fleeing this sacred place.

7. Sit down and, beginning at your feet, cover yourself with the earth material. Leave your face clear but put a symbolic bit of material on your forehead. Continue praying or chanting the whole time.

Note: Salt is such a potent banishing material that it is not necessary to cover yourself with it. If using rock salt for this ritual, simply lie down on a layer of it, sprinkle it, or even just step in it with your bare feet.

8. Lie quietly. Sink into the earth and a deep meditative state. be silent. Visualize all the negative forces swirling about you sinking into the earth, deep, deep into the planet. As you breathe in, see the healing and banishing green power of the earth fill you. Do this for at least ten minutes, longer if possible.

9. When done, slowly arise as one reborn.

10. Loudly declare, with prayers, chants, or other power words, that you are free of the negative forces. Declare that any left over negative forces are now fixed in and absorbed by the earth. Visualize this.

11. Bury the used earth material. Shake out the blanket, if you were using one.

12. Afterwards, in the lying-down spot carefully bury something (a bit of hair is traditional or maybe a token of what you are banishing), thanking Mother Earth.

Banishing with Sprinkled Earth

This banishing ritual is similar to the previous one, except that instead of lying in earth or covering your body with earth you are systematically sprinkling earth over a whole area or home. "Sacred earth" or "fixing powders" are often sold in botanikas or New Age/occult stores; they are part Santeria, Voodoo, and Candoble rituals. You may want to experiment with these. Rock salt and crushed herbs are also famous for banishing negative forces; both can be bought as is. Other traditions stress the banishing use of leaves or boughs (oak, pine) or ferns or grasses (like sweetgrass).

Preparations:

• Choose the herb or salt or other materials you wish to use and charge them, using focus, will, intent, and suitable prayers or chants.

• Make sure that whatever material you use is freshly gathered, has no chemicals in or on it, and comes from a positive source. If you are gathering herbs, leaves, or ferns, it is traditional to offer the contributing plant a small thank you. Be thoughtful, creative, focused, and look at the appendix for ideas on personality or creatively shifting your banishing work.

• Have the crushed fresh herbs, salt, leaves, or whatever in a container of some sort. Make sure the area to be cleared has been swept clean.

Procedure:

1. Open the container with prayers or chants. Offer some of your material to the earth and sprinkle a bit at the entrance of the dwelling or room.

2. Hold the container up to each of the four directions and sprinkle a bit to north, east, south, and west with suitable prayers or chants.

3. Meditate on the cleansing properties of earth. Bless yourself with the earth material by touching a bit of it to your head, heart, and loins while praying or chanting. If you are banishing with someone else, have him or her do the same.

4. Going counterclockwise, circle the area and sprinkle the material all over while praying or chanting. Strongly visualize the negative forces fleeing and/or being absorbed by the earth material. Do this around the whole area three times.

5. Leave the affected area for several hours; a full day is even better.

6. Return with a broom. Facing north, say a prayer or chant. Working counterclockwise, slowly, carefully, and systematically sweep all of the material out of the room or dwelling. Sweep it all out the door. Gather all the material into a bag using a dustpan.

7. Carry the swept-up material outside, bury all of it in the earth, then throw the bag away in the garbage. Touch the earth and let all the leftover negative energy be absorbed.

8. Return to the cleared area and loudly declare (and visualize) the place free of all negative or evil influences.

Banishing with Trees and Plants

Using trees for banishing is a very ancient and pervasive idea that is still widely practiced in a number of places. The idea is so deeply entrenched even in our culture that we don't realize it. Most cemeteries have trees, but few realize that trees were originally planted near graves to keep ghosts away, to purify the area, and as a way to connect with the deceased. Birch trees, seen as banishing ignorance and evil in ancient Norse tradition, are often planted near schools even today, though most have forgotten why. We still knock on wood for luck, a practice that goes far back into Pagan cultures where tree spirits were known as powerful beings. Today, no one argues the positive affects trees and forests have on people and the planet. This banishing practice taps into the idea that trees are material beings as well as complex energy systems and that they spiritually purify areas as well as purify the air.

Procedure 1 (Personal Banishing): Find the healthiest, biggest, and nicest tree you can. The kind of tree that can symbolically connect with what you want to banish. For weakness you may want to use an oak, for example. See the appendix for ideas.

1. Hold the tree with both hands and put your forehead on it. Close your eyes. Open yourself to the tree. See if it is the "right" tree for you, if it matches your personal energy. Maybe even ask the tree for help in banishing.

2. If this is the right tree, then turn around and lean against it with your full spine or sit at the base of the tree in this way.

3. Pray or chant and breathe deeply and rhythmically. Fully relax your whole body. As you breathe out, see the negative forces flow out of you and down into the tree's roots. As you breathe in, feel and see the energy of the tree flowing from the leaves down into the tree and into you. Do this for as long as possible.

4. When done, pray or chant and acknowledge that the negative force is gone.

5. Hold the tree and thank it and the Mother Earth.

6. Leave some token of yourself buried at the base of the tree.

Procedure 2 (Planting Banishing): Another banishing can be done by planting trees (or other important banishing plants, like rosemary or holly) in areas that are negative or have negative influences. Traditionally such guardian trees neutralize and actively repel evil.

First, choose the right banishing plant or tree (see the appendix). Make sure it is healthy and not saturated with chemicals. Also make sure you know how and where to plant it so it will prosper.

1. Clear the area and yourself before the planting. Have everything (compost, spade, water, pre-dug hole) ready before you begin.

2. Bless the area and operation with a prayer, chant, or other sacred words.

3. Plant the tree, bush, or plant.

4. As you push the dirt down with both hands, pray or chant about exactly what you want this plant to do. Visualize it happening.

5. Water the plant thoroughly. Thank it and the Mother Earth.

6. Water and pray or chant over the plant for the next three days. On the last day, pray or chant and declare the bad energy gone or repelled.

Note: Consider planting a charm, amulet, special stone, or symbolic item with the plant. Trouble with a neighbor, for example, might be banished by planting the nasty note from the neighbor in a hole with a holly bush facing the neighbor's house. If you do decide to plant something with the tree or bush, charge it beforehand.

Banishing with Stones and Crystals

Some of the earliest prehistoric charms, found in Cro-Magnon graves, were crystals, and any visit to a museum will show that every culture has believed in the magical power of stones and minerals. Using crystals, precious and semiprecious stones, and other rocks and stones for energy work and healing is so popular today that only basic banishing procedures are outlined here. When using stones and crystals for banishing, keep the following in mind.

- First, know where the stones and crystals came from and who has been handling or shaping them. Origins count, and stones and crystals are said to imprint energies.

- Even if you feel good about the stones you are using, clear them of other energies. This can be done by simply putting them in salt for a time.

- Use the appropriate gem, crystal, or stone for what you are banishing. (See the appendix for ideas.) For example, carnelian is good for banishing pain traditionally, but garnet is not.

- In many magical traditions, holy stones call to a person from the ocean or a river. Stones you find this way or that otherwise feel "right" are great for banishing. Found stones with holes in them are said to be power objects.

   Procedure 1 (Personal Healing): Place the stone on the afflicted body part (or chakra). Or for general banishing, begin with it on the forehead and move it down the whole body. As with all other banishings, clean and clear yourself beforehand; pray or chant and add any other ritual flourishes you like. There should be silent period of relaxing and visualizing the stone banishing or absorbing the negative forces. *Always* clean the stone in salt or running water afterwards to dump the negative energies collected.

   Procedure 2 (Banishing an Area of Negative Energy): Follow the same basic procedures as set out for the "Banishing with Sprinkled Earth" ritual, except instead of sprinkling, simply hold the stone in both hands. Walk counterclockwise around the area three times and visualize the stone sucking up the negative energies or blasting them away. Then leave the stone in the center of the area or space for a time.

When done, bury the stone for a time outside. If you want to reuse it, dig it up and wash it in running water and place it in some salt to clear it. After that, wrap it in clean cloth until next time.

Note: You can also simply toss away the stone after using it to absorb negative energy. One technique is to write or draw a symbol of the banished energy on the rock and then toss it away (perhaps over a cliff or into the ocean) with suitable prayers or chants. Use your imagination!

Earth Activities for Spiritual Banishing

These activities are associated with the banishing power of earth, deep power, solidity, grounding, the ancestors, darkness, nature, fertility, and the healing power of earth-spirit energies.

• Hiking

• Mountain or cliff climbing

• Exploring caves, meditating in caves

• Rock hunting

• Stretching and stabilizing exercises

• Slower forms of tai chi and chi gong

• Sculpting

• Gardening

• Building

• Hard cleaning

• Toolmaking

To use these activities for banishing, follow the general procedure described at the beginning of the chapter.

Procedure: After focusing on your problem and intent, centering yourself and so on, find a suitable time/place to perform the action.

- Offer appropriate prayer/chants etc. and visualize/call forth the banishing power of stone, earth, trees, and all green Gaia energy, feel the solidity and the vibrant beating heart of the Earth beneath you, let it fill and still you.

- Do the action with full focus, visualization, and a constant tape loop prayer or chant or affirmation.

- At the peak experience, let go of the negative energy. Feel/see it sink deep into the dark earth and stones beneath you, like a plant with deep roots. Let all negativity flow down into the earth. Be calm and at peace!

- Affirm this fact. Be centered like a mountain in peace for a moment. With both hands, feel the earth beneath you, supporting and nourishing you. Give thanks.

- When done, sprinkle a pinch of soil on the earth with thanks, end the rite.

Earth Tools for Spiritual Banishing

Stones, crystals, gems, jewels: Entire books can and have been written on the spiritual powers of these things. The charts in the appendix give specific banishing correspondences. These earth tools often take the form of sacred jewelry, which has for eons been worn for both empowerment and banishing. Crystals are often used as wands to direct force. The Vajra (thunderbolt), a prevalent divine symbol in several cultures (both Shiva and Zeus have one), was likely originally a double crystal. Stones and crystals can be used as focus points in meditation, for scrying or seeking visions in, or as part of another item (such as a staff, dagger hilt, or chalice). Or they can simply to be kept in the pocket for everyday energy work, including banishing.

Pentacle: The traditional tool of earth is the pentacle, a dishlike circle. It represents earth as well as the planet earth. In various spiritual traditions, it has different symbols on it, from a pentagram to a cross. Pentacles (or patens) are made of stone, clay, wood, metal, or some other earth-based substance. In most ritual traditions, the pentacle or plate is what offerings are placed upon. It is the tool used in earthing energy or for charging an item with positive energy.

Orb, globe: The circle or globe is a deep image of wholeness and of the earth. It has been used in ritual and architecture for centuries. Kings and queens traditionally held an orb or globe in one hand to show their dominion over the world. Later a cross was added to the top of it in Christian kingdoms.

Seat or throne: Traditionally the seat was the place of power for kings, magicians, shamans, and so on. In many traditions, where you sit, especially when meditating or doing spiritual energy work, becomes a place of great power and gathers spiritual force. Often the seat or throne of a king, guru, or person of power is venerated long after that person is gone. It is traditional to have your own cushion or seat—a seat that is only used by you—when doing energy work. Often square (a symbol of earth), this seat denotes stability, power, and centeredness.

Tree: The Tree of Life is one of the few truly universal symbols that transcends polytheism, monotheism, cultures, and countries. While it is not exactly a tool, spiritual healers and practitioners often have special trees of power they use for specific things. Trees are used for banishing, used as spiritual batteries to hold spiritual forces for later work, and are often seen as entities that are valuable allies.

Several traditions have a tree in the center of their temple (or a pillar representing a tree) as the *axis mundi* about which all spins. Items made from special or sacred trees are powerful tools.

Pyramid: Pyramids take the powerful, stable earth form of a square and focus it to a point. There are so many mysteries and marvels associated with pyramids that I will leave it to you to explore their deeper esoteric meaning on your own. However, as a tool, made of metal, stone, crystal, or other earth-based substance, they are said to concentrate spiritual energy. They can also be used to charge items and apparently even sharpen razor blades. Some people have reported that sitting in a pyramid form actually banishes negative energies.

Key Earth Symbols for Spiritual Banishing

Symbol	Meaning
Tree	The universe, growth, protection, strength, life
Circle (or circle with a cross in the center)	The world, the earth, grounding, centering, the four quarters
Mountain	Strength, power, stability, heaven and earth, gods
Square (and cube)	A throne, stability, earth, worldly power, balance
Pyramid	Similar to mountain; focused stability, divinity
Cross (equal-armed)	The center of the world, balance, centering, the four quarters
Globe, orb	Deep image of wholeness, the earth

Spirit

In spiritual banishing, the "greater mind" must concentrate and, on a very deep level, transform outward ritual actions into meaningful spiritual actions with deep reverberating symbolic power. Everyone who does specific spiritual practices to banish is looking to affect the mundane world by using intangibles such as will, love, and imagination.

There are endless ways to do this, but the key to any spiritual banishing—whether you're using ritual techniques or practices that manipulate air, earth, fire, or water—is your intent or will. And simply using will or focused real intent is not enough unless it is backed up with love—love for the Self, love for others, love for the state you wish to be in, and love for the world in which we live. The act of love combined with this spiritual focus can banish or change anything.

Purely spiritual banishing requires no symbol, no tool, and no real lengthy ritual or procedure. Often a person who is attuned to the given situation can make small adjustments in reality and so sidestep any negative entity or being. Spiritually centered practices such as tai chi emphasize this idea of *wei wu wei* or "nothing doing nothing."

In fact, if one begins with the reality framework that all is illusion, then there is really no difference between this or that energy, and a positive force in the wrong place or time may easily be seen as a negative force. This moral ambiguity underlies much of Eastern mysticism, and therefore the concept of banishing can change with perspective. Most of this book assumes a reality framework that says "X is good, but Y is bad, therefore we will encourage X and banish Y." From a pragmatic point of view, this idea works well, but in the end, understanding, letting go, or working through is a better and more lasting strategy for banishing than simply commanding something to go. A pain may be a good thing if it alerts you to a larger problem. Stress is sometimes a positive thing if we are indeed working through something that is difficult. Fear is often a positive reaction to a real threat and, as such, helps us survive and learn and grow.

The purely spiritual view of banishing is this: everything is part of a larger whole or pattern. Everything exists to teach us something. Banishing cannot be avoiding. Instead, it should be a conscious correcting, balancing, or adjusting.

And so here are a number of purely spiritual techniques that can be used for banishing. They can be used in any way, shape, or form, so no step-by-step procedures will be listed. They are all useful for knowing and becoming aware, which is, of course, the ultimate banishing of all negativity.

Visualization: Sacred Images

Often a sacred image, clearly and powerfully visualized, is enough to banish negative forces. The key is to use a symbol with deep and powerful spiritual meaning to you. A simple line-figure symbol is best. Visualize it clearly in the center of darkness, glowing with the light of pure love. The light grows in intensity until it fills every corner of your mind and of the space around you. Clarity, focus, and will are crucial here.

Some common symbols used this way are the Om symbol, a cross, a five-pointed star, a star of David, a crescent moon, a sun, or an eye in a triangle.

Vibration: Sacred Sounds

In many cosmologies it is pure vibration that created the universe. "In the beginning was the Word," says the New Testament. In Hinduism, Om is the origin and ending of the universe; in Cabala, it is the vibration of

IHVH. Sacred sounds or syllables are key banishing tools that can be used with great affect.

Again, the key is meditative focus, a strong will, and the pouring of pure love into and through the sound. The sound originates in the center of all things and expands outward in growing ripples of pure power and creation to banish any negative forces.

While the sound can come from an instrument (such as a bell), it is often uttered by the banisher. A sacred syllable like Om should be vibrated after a deep breath, arise from the base of the body up through the whole body, and thus vibrate the whole body and the universe. Other common vibration syllables include *Allah*, *Iao*, *lux*, *pax*, *Gam* (the god Ganesh), *Krim* (the goddess Kali), and *phat* (the lightening bolt banishing).

All the world's religions offer many mantras or sacred sentences that can be powerful tools for defeating negative forces. Latin phrases (such as *lux fiat*, "Let there be light"), special phrases from the Talmud and the Koran, and special mantras embodying the powers of the various gods and goddesses of Hinduism are some examples. Even a simple affirmation (such as "all you need is love") can become a powerful banishing vibration if imbued with enough will and love and executed with keen focus. Research your spiritual tradition and find what you need.

Gesture: Sacred Hand and Body Movements

Making a gesture (like placing the palms together) can be a simple reflex or an explosive and powerful banishing technique, depending on how you do it. The power is not in the gesture itself, but in the intent and the focus of personal and spiritual power through will as love.

In Buddhism, Hinduism, and Tantrika such powerful hand gestures are very important in ritual and meditation. One of the most common ways to banish with gesture is to simply raise up a hand, palm out. This is the gesture (mudra) of dispelling fear. In Islamic countries, touching the heart projects the love of God. Full body gestures (such as yoga postures) are also powerful tools for banishing. Stepping forward and throwing the arms straight out—the sign of Horus the Enterer—is a powerful, focused posture used to project spiritual force.

Whatever posture or gesture you do, see it as the center of the cosmos, the unspoken signal to utterly change the universe. Feel the effect echoing out like a clap of thunder or a physical gust of wind, banishing all within and around you.

Some common gestures are the sign of the lotus (hands cupped together, fingers up and open, thumbs and pinkies touching), the sign of the cross, the sign of blessing (hand up, index and middle fingers raised, the rest folded), the sign of the horns (thumb and pinky raised, the rest folded), the sign of surrendering to god (hands and arms up), the mudra of the sword (same as the sign of blessing, but held in front of the chest), and the sign of bliss (one hand raised, thumb and index finger touching).

Energy Work: Sacred Shakti

The purest form of banishing is silent energy work. All the great sages, saints, prophets, holy men, shamans, and priests or priestesses are said to be able to make things happen simply by the force of their power, their shakti or emanation. One definition of magick (by A. O. Spare) that I particularly like is "the ability to get without asking." Truly enlightened masters of all religions would agree that pure awareness, being, unity with God banishes all negative forces. Awakening to spiritual truth is full and complete awareness that God is love and that the universe is wholly right, pure, and divine.

Of course, achieving this illumination is easier said (or written) than done.

Yet flashes of this elevated consciousness (sometimes called *gnosis*) can be generated through awareness and projection of pure energy. The pure form of this consciousness is more dependant on a specific mindset rather than a visualization, vibration, or gesture. You concentrate and focus on the powerful energetic body you have, you enflame your energy field (aura) through focused will and love, and you either raise it up your body from base of spine to the top of your head, or simply light up the whole core of your being and project it out as an explosion of pure force to banish all evil.

Often this energy is built up and generated before this "aura explosion" through a number of different means. Some of the most common include dancing, intense prayer, exercise, sex, chakra work, spinning, or any number of other ritual practices.

Centering: Sacred Altars

Altars are places that emanate divine energy to both bless and protect. It makes sense, in terms of spiritual banishing, to have a shrine or alter in your home no matter what your faith. An altar is a place between the spirit world and the normal world, a place where the two touch and merge. A deity is called down to the altar (or to wards, protective statues or images, usually set up by doors) and so is always present to project and fill the area with the divine. So simply being near an altar banishes negative energy.

Going to a church, shrine, temple, or other holy spot can banish negativity. Meditating in front of a Buddha image can banish.

Again, much depends on your focused power and the will and love you have charged the altar with. The altar should be facing a particular direction, depending on your faith. It may be portable (a rug, cushion, or image) or may be a fixture. Continually charging or reinforcing the spiritual power in the altar will increase its effectiveness and intensity.

Some common things found on altars are symbols of the four elements (incense or a flower for air; a candle or lamp for fire; a cup or vessel of liquid for water; fruit, flowers, or food for earth; a symbol or image of a key for spirit), elemental tools (such as a wand, sword, cup, pentacle or stone, and deity image), spiritual symbols or images (a cross; a statue of a saint, the Goddess, or Buddha; a crystal; a menorah; and so on) and often holy books (the Rig Veda, Bible, Koran, Torah, Book of Shadows, Tao The King, or Diamond Sutra).

In parting, let me say this: Your life is your own. You exist for a reason and the journey of life is to discover what exactly your Path is and then to follow it. Banishing is, in the end, a way to assist you in doing this thing. Banishing can help you avoid errors, balance imbalances, make corrections and remove hindrances that are negatively impacting your True Will, your Path. You have personal power and the universe behind you, but it is easy to "fall asleep" and let others make decisions for you. In the end, the only real way to banish those things afflicting you is to first take back control of your life, assert your True Will, accept and express Love as a daily practice and then banish those things that keep you from a balanced life, the life you really and truly deserve: happiness, awareness, and compassion.

Have fun!

Appendix: Charts and Correspondences

Timing a Banishing

Timing, it is said, is everything.

In spiritual traditions all over the earth, ritual items are often gathered, created, or prepared at specific times to add potency to the intended operation. Actual banishing work is also said to be best done at certain times. Here are some common times said to be good for such things:

Best time of day:

midnight

high noon

the depth of the night: 1–4am

dawn or twilight

Best time of month:

the new moon night

the week between the last quarter of the moon & new moon

Best time of year:

Misrule: the liminal time period between December 24 and January 6

In general: both equinoxes and both solstices

Lammas (Aug 1), especially for fire banishing

Halloween (Oct 31), also called Samhain

the days leading up to the Winter Solstice (Yule)

New Year's Eve, New Year's Day

Best Astrological Signs:

Each astrological sign is said to be particularly good for specific kinds of banishings. Here are some of the traditional attributes:

Sign	Best for banishing:
Aries (March 20–April 20)	procrastination, low energy, depression, repressed anger
Taurus (April 21–May 21)	physical issues, money problems, personal environment problems
Gemini (May 22–June 22)	over-organization, closed emotions or mind, creative blocks, lack of creativity, boredom, depression
Cancer (June 23–July 22)	emotional issues, anxiety and worry problems, feeling issues, oversensitivity, professional and career issues
Leo (July 23–August 22)	ego issues, authoritarian/ anger/aggressive issues, issues involving politics, power, and confidence
Virgo (August 23–September 23)	timidity, relationship issues, health issues, self-worth feelings, indecision issues, repression issues, and concentration

Libra (September 23–October 22)	imbalances of all kinds, lust, codependence, creative blocks
Scorpio (October 23–November 22)	deep psychological issues, sexual issues, insomnia, overactive mind, emotional issues, communication issues, health issues
Sagittarius (November 23–December 22)	hyperactivity, mind flightiness, negative moods, egoism, overaggressiveness, political issues, mental and physical balance
Capricorn (December 23–January 21)	business or money issues, cleanliness/organizational issues, physical health issues, temper and other emotional/mental-regulating issues, concentration and focus issues
Aquarius (January 22–February 20)	issues of disconnection (get grounded!), emotional issues, overempathizing, relationship issues, intellectual/mental issues/fixations
Pisces (February 21–March 19)	emotional pains, the blues, emotional and mental overwhelm, self-confidence, self-awareness, lack of assertiveness, focus and mental organization issues

Items and Substances to Use

Important: Read before using!

1. The spiritual powers and properties ascribed to the following items is based on folklore, historical sources, and indigenous traditions. No claim is made by the author concerning the usefulness or "magick" of these items! So much of spiritual banishing in many different cultures around the globe seems to depend on belief and traditional schemas. Certain items may cause verifiable effects (lavender scent has been shown to induce relaxation, for example), but energetic or spiritual effectiveness is absolutely in the eye of the banisher!

   Note: A number of these items (herbs, fruit) can be ingested. Chamomile and mint make fine teas, for example. However, *do not ingest any of the herbs mentioned in any way unless you are either certain that they are safe to eat or have checked with a healthcare provider.*

   All the items here are listed here purely for ritual use.

2. A number of items may be used in more than one way. This is why they are not listed under specific elements of Air, Fire, Water, or Earth. Lavender, for example, may be hung over the doorway or burned as smoke to banish (air), used to build or added to a small banishing fire (fire), used in a banishing bath, applied as a banishing oil, or used to make a banishing wash (water). It can be planted in front of a home to banish evil (earth) or useful in sachets and pillows for meditation and dream work (Spirit). Always use what is appropriate in an appropriate manner after appropriate preparation.

   I will often note traditional uses of an herb or other substance (scents, oils, washes, sachets, incenses, and so on). This depends on what information I have available or the limitations of space. If I don't list a substance's specific powers or uses, use your judgment.

For instance, if I call for an herb you are not familiar with, do a bit of research on it first. Seek out information. Experiment a bit and be sure you (or anyone else involved in the banishing) is not allergic to it. You might want to burn a little first or make a small wash (a tea or infusion used for washing) in a cup before bathing in it or filling your home with the fumes! If in doubt, stick with a nice safe herb that you are absolutely sure is fine: lavendar, garlic, rosemary, etc.

Important: Anything marked with an X is a noxious substance. In other words it will have a nasty smell, might be harmful if ingested or cause a skin reaction. etc. Only burn a little of such an herb when banishing, with open windows, and don't use for bathing, smoking, etc.

Do your homework, use your judgment, start small, and discover the powers of spiritual banishing for yourself. All, with Love & Will!

—Denny Sargent

Stones

Stone	Banishing Properties
Amber	Excellent for banishing all kinds of ills. It is one of the oldest protective stones. Also for banishing "the blues" and increasing happiness.
Amethyst	Great for banishing all spiritual and emotional problems, to create balance or harmony, as well as for banishing digestion problems.
Carnelian	A very powerful protection/banishing stone valued by the Egyptians, among others. Banishes pain away, relieves all sorts of symptoms and aches.

Citrine	Useful for banishing spinal work and to manipulate all kinds of energy work.
Coral	Banishes negative emotions and strengthens one's emotional foundation.
Diamonds	Banishes everything—the power of pure "light." A very intense stone, it increases the power of other stones.
Emerald	For banishing ills of the body and heart, and for emotional healing. A very powerful healing focus stone.
Jade	A stone famous all over Asia for banishing evil, healing, banishing bad luck, and purifying everything.
Lapis	Good for all heart healing and banishing issues affecting one mentally, emotionally, and physically.
Malachite	An excellent stone for banishing anything preventing a prosperous and healthy environment, for strengthening the physical body, for earthing energies, and for restoring harmony into one's life.
Moonstone	Great for emotional banishing, dream work banishing, cleansing and clearing energy blocks, and is said to balance yin/yang.
Black Obsidian	Great for protection and clearing, as well as revealing and banishing underlying causes of problems.

Black Onyx	A wonderful stone for protection, banishing evil, and grounding of negative feeling or energies.
Opal	This is a powerful active healing stone that banishes physical ills and is used to promote circulation and heal the nerves, as well as open up the energy centers.
Freshwater Pearl	Banishes love problems and heals skin and emotional problems.
Quartz	This stone is great for all kinds of banishing— it is one of the earliest stones found, used by Neanderthals, and has been used in banishing ever since. It is said to be healing, especially of flesh, bones, muscle, and so on. Different kinds promote different forms of healing. Quartz healing stones have been used for thousands of years all over the world.
Rose Quartz	A great stone for banishing emotional imbalance, as well as any blood or stamina problems. A wonderful loving, healing stone.
Ruby	A pure banishing energy stone, quite fiery, good for bringing energy and immune system power to bear on a health problem. Great for inciting passion and power in all banishing work.
Sapphire	This stone is great for banishing excessiveness, cooling an overactive system, for bringing a gentleness to the healing process, and for promoting banishing fatigue.
Sodalite	This stone protects one from negative energy.

Metals and Miscellaneous

Metal	Banishing Property
Salt	The single most agreed upon banishing substance. In virtually every culture, salt is said to banish evil of all kinds, from spirits to death. Peoples all over banish ritually with salt. You can: step in it, sprinkle it, leave piles of it, eat it, bathe in it, make a circle of it, even burn it!
Sulpher	Having dark connotations, sulpher (especially burning it) is said to banish infernal spirits. (X)
Iron	Wearing, carrying, or having things made of iron is said to repel and banish all things of magick, from demons to faerie.
Gold	The "highest" metal and so banishes, as the sun banishes, physical, mental, and emotional problems, as well as spiritual entities and forces.
Silver	More a metal of the moon, used to banish shadow and dream creatures and nightmares of all kinds. Think silver bullets . . .
Lead	The dark and heavy metal of Saturn is said to banish by earthing, fixing, or "sinking" evil. Handle and use this metal carefully, never burn, never ingest. (X)
Clay	Daubed on bodies, walls and floors, clay of all colors is used to spiritually banish, cleanse, and artistically form symbols in rituals used to protect or banish. White, red, yellow, and black are the most common clays.

Meteorite	Clears away evil.	

Herbs

Herb	Banishing Properties	Best Uses
Angelica	Banishes/purifies evil	sprinkled about the home (4 quarters)
Asafetida	Banishes evil, demons, malignant spirits with foul odor (X)	burned (a little)
Bamboo	Protects places, banishes harmful forces	planted, placed
Basil	Averts evil, protects against and banishes evil entities	burned
Burdock	Banishes evil and protects person/place	all ways
Cactus	Planted nearby, banishes and deflects evil (X)	planted, placed
Chamomile	Removes negative forces, banishes bad luck	tea/bath
Caraway	Protects against and banishes evil entities	burned/placed
Clove	Banishes evil	burned or hung
Cumin	Averts evil	burned
Dill	Banishes evil and protects person/place	eaten, planted or hung

Elder	Banishes evil and protects person/place	branches hung
Fennel	Binds (absorbs) negative energies	all ways
Garlic	Averts evil, especially when used on Fridays; Clears evil away by presence	burned
Geranium	Protects home and banishes vermin, evil forces, and bad feelings	all ways
Ginger Fern	Banishes evil, removes negative energy	burned (to rid evil), present (to remove negative energy)
Hyssop	Purifies evil, clears away negativity, banishes "curses"	bath, burned or sprinkled
Lavender	This key herb does everything: banishes discord, bad health, evil etc.	Used all ways: fresh, dried, sachets, etc.
Lemon Verbena	Purifies and cleans of negativity	wash/bath/tea
Marjoram	Banishes negativity and the blues	dried and fresh forms, as wash/tea
Mint	Banishes evil entities, poverty, negative feelings	burned, planted, or as wash

Mistletoe	Banishes evil	hung or burned
Mugwort	Very powerful banishing/ protective herb, psychic, dream, energy banishings (X)	hung, as sachets
Mullein	Powerful banisher of evil energies, nightmares, and people	hung, as sachets, burned
Nettle Leaves	Banishes evil, ghosts, and ill health	burned, scattered, in bath (X) Caution: can sting!
Pennyroyal	Banishes bad vibes, evil	hung, carried, burned. Never ingest. (X)
Pepper, Black	Banishes evil; clears evil away, returns evil	burned, present
Pepper, Red (Chili)	Banishes and repels evil	scattered or burned
Peppermint	Clears evil away, banishes ill will, and bad feelings	all ways
Rose	Key herb for emotional/ health banishing	all ways
Rosemary	Averts evil, protects against and banishes negative influences	all ways
Rue	Clears evil away, protects when carried, banishes "curses"	burned or wash

Sage	A key herb in protecting, banishing, repelling evil, curses, negative energies, etc.	all ways
St. John's Wort	Protects and banishes evil energies, removes evil influences	worn, planted
Sweetgrass	Used as sage by many Native Americans to banish negativity of all kinds	burned/hung
Thistle	Aggressively banishes evil and protects person/place	grown, hung, burned (X)
Thyme	A key herb for banishing negative spirits, feelings, ills of all kinds	used as incense; /bath/tea/carried
Tobacco (and Indian tobacco)	Banishes all spirits/ vibes/energies	burned, always use pure form (X!)
Vervain	Averts evil, emotional stress, negative feelings of all kinds, and purifies	carried, burned, juice
Wormwood	Banishes negativity, evil entities, and curses	burned (X)
Yarrow	Banishes evil and protects person/place	present, burned, and as wash

Woods, Resins, Flowers, Foods

Substance	Properties	Best Uses
Birch	Repels negativity and evil	planted near, branch hung, burned
Blackberry vine & flowers	Banishes and repels/ returns evil	hung, burned
Cedar	Banishes evil, removes negativity, protects	burned bark, branches; present
Daffodil	Banishes evil and protects person/place	live plant in home
Dragon's Blood	Protects against and banishes evil entities (X)	burned, carried to protect
Egg	Binds or removes/purifies negative energies	rubbed on a person, tossed
Fern	Banishes evil, removes negative energy	planted nearby, burned fronds swept
Frankincense	Key and powerful resin, banishes all negativity and evil	burned/carried
Hawthorn	Protects against and banishes negative influences	branch hung, burned

Hemlock	Banishes evil	grown nearby or placed (X!)
Holly	Banishes evil and protects person/place	planted, branches present (Never burn!)
Honeysuckle	Averts evil, banishes fevers	hand a loop to banish illness
Hyacinth	Banishes nightmares/bad feelings/the blues	fresh/dried, as a wash
Ivy	Banishes and protects against evil	planted or hung (X)
Juniper	Key banisher, banishes evil forces and protects (X)	burned/carried, hung over door
Leeks	Banishes and protects	grown, hung, carried, or eaten
Lemon	Powerful banisher; banishes all negativity and "old" vibes	juice/fruit/scent
Lilac	Banishes all having to do with the dead, averts evil	placed/carried (Don't burn)
Marigolds	Banishes ill health, the blues	live/dried flowers, as wash/tea, etc.
Myrrh	Banishes negativity especially in objects, or in healing	burned/carried
Oak	Powerful banisher; banishes evils, draws away evil	Acorns/wood carried; planted, hung, or burned

Onion	Banishes by absorbing negativity	cut in half to absorb evil
Orange	Banishes negative feelings and thoughts, emotional problems	scent/fruit/juice
Pine	Protects against and banishes evil entities, hides place/person from evil	burned, hung, planted
Pumpkin	Banishes supernatural evils and poverty	placed in rooms, by doors
Rowen (Mountain Ash)	Protects against evil energies and entities	planted or branches hung
Sandalwood	Very powerful banisher and protector, used for eons	burned or carried as beads
Willow	Key banisher, averts and protects against evil	planted nearby, a loop hung
Yew	Averts evil (X)	planted, boughs hung

Other Liquids Used to Banish

Water: spring, ocean, river, waterfall, lake, rain, and "fixed" water, is water to which a gem, metal, or other spiritually charged substance has been added for a period of time, thus "charging" it. Example: A magnet can be added to a jar of water for a period time (a month), thus charging it. This water is then said to have special banishing powers. **Alcohol:** Rum, Vodka, Brandy

Florida Water: a common cologne found in many Botanikas or New Age stores. Protects against and banishes evil or negative energies from others.

Oils/tinctures/extractions: from herbs, plants, and resins (see previous lists)*

Other Solids Used to Banish

Pollen (from a variety of plants, corn being very common)

Feathers or feather down

Dusts, dirts from sacred places

Bones or parts of bones, teeth

Leaves, fronds, branches, nuts, seeds (see previous list of plants)

Amulets, scriptures, holy books, holy objects

Hair, fur

To Our Readers

Weiser Books, an imprint of Red Wheel/Weiser, publishes books across the entire spectrum of occult and esoteric subjects. Our mission is to publish quality books that will make a difference in people's lives without advocating any one particular path or field of study. We value the integrity, originality, and depth of knowledge of our authors.

Our readers are our most important resource, and we appreciate your input, suggestions, and ideas about what you would like to see published. Please feel free to contact us, to request our latest book catalog, or to be added to our mailing list.

Red Wheel/Weiser, LLC
500 Third Street, Suite 230
San Francisco, CA 94107
www.redwheelweiser.com

About the Author

Denny Sargent (aka Aion, Hermeteicusnath) is an eclectic ritualist and a member of a number of initiatory magick groups. Today the Western Magickal Tradition, Tantrika, and Taoism form increasingly important foci for his studies and writing. He is the author of *Your Guardian Angel and You, The Tao of Birth Days,* and *The Magical Garden,* which he wrote with his wife Sophia. He has contributed to a number of magazines, including *PanGaia* and *Green Egg.* He and his wife live in Seattle.

Visit him at *http://www.psychicsophia.com/cleansweep.html.*